Passive Wealth, Active Happiness

Mastering the Art of Effortless Income

By
Josephine Goody

Passive Wealth, Active Happiness

Mastering the Art of Effortless Income

Contents

Why Passive Income Is the Key to Your Freedom

Imagine waking up on a lazy Sunday morning, the sun streaming through your window. You pour yourself a cup of coffee and glance at your phone. Notifications flood in, not from your boss or your job, but alerts telling you that you made money while you were sleeping. It's like the modern-day version of finding gold. This isn't a fairy tale; it's the reality of passive income.

Passive income means earning money without the need for active involvement, allowing you to focus on what you love instead of just what pays the bills. It's about unlocking the potential to live life on your own terms, whether that's traveling the world, pursuing personal passions, or simply having more time with family and friends. Your life is no longer tethered to the demands of a 9-to-5 job. The concept may sound a bit fantastical, but let's dive deeper to see why it's not just attainable but transformative.

Freedom. It's a powerful word that resonates deeply with everyone. Passive income gives you that freedom. Financial stability is no longer an elusive dream but a tangible, achievable goal. No more counting the days until your next paycheck, worrying about how to cover bills, or limiting your life experiences due to financial constraints. Passive income provides the foundation to build a life filled with options.

However, achieving this freedom requires a strategic approach. It's not about quitting your job today and hoping for the best. It involves careful planning, prudent investments, and a bit of hustle upfront. But once set in motion, passive income streams can grow and sustain themselves with minimal effort, allowing you to reap the rewards for years to come.

Imagine having revenue streams that function like several pillars of support. Whether it's through real estate investments, dividend stocks, or online businesses, you have multiple ways to keep your financial ship steady. When done correctly, these streams operate harmoniously and even compensate for each other during economic fluctuations.

Why is passive income crucial for your freedom? It changes the game completely, putting the power back in your hands. No longer do you need to trade your most finite resource—time—for money. Traditional employment binds you to a schedule, a location, and often, someone else's rules. Passive income breaks those chains.

Think about the possibilities. Want to spend six months learning to surf in Hawaii? You can. Fancy taking a sabbatical to write that novel you've always dreamed of? Go for it. Passive income doesn't just grant financial freedom; it grants time. Suddenly, you have the bandwidth to explore your interests, deepen relationships, and live more fully.

It's essential to distinguish passive income from get-rich-quick schemes. Passive income strategies require diligence, education, and often a mentor. Get-rich-quick schemes promise unrealistic returns with minimal effort and usually lead to disappointment and financial loss. Successful passive income is built on sound investments and well-thought-out plans.

Moreover, passive income allows you to be proactive rather than reactive. In traditional work settings, your income is at the mercy of external factors—economic downturns, corporate restructures, or even technology taking over jobs. Passive income gives you a financial buffer and autonomy, making you resilient against unforeseen changes in the job market or economy.

Imagine diversifying your income through real estate investments, dividend stocks, and online businesses. This diversification not only stabilizes your financial situation but also brings a sense of security. You no longer have to put all your eggs in one basket. If one revenue stream falters, others can keep you afloat.

What's more, the initial groundwork you put into building passive income streams can yield compounding returns. For instance, investing in dividend stocks can provide you with periodic payouts, which can be reinvested to generate even more income. The same goes for online businesses; an initial time investment to set up can lead to exponential growth as your audience and revenue streams expand.

One of the biggest advantages of passive income is the mental freedom it provides. Financial stress is one of the most significant stressors people face. With passive income, you alleviate a huge portion of that stress. You're no longer living paycheck to paycheck, constantly worried about job security or unexpected expenses. This reduction in stress leads to more mental clarity, better health, and overall improved quality of life.

Many might argue that pursuing passive income sounds good on paper but is challenging in practice. They're not wrong, but all worthwhile endeavors come with their challenges. The key is persistence, education, and leveraging the right opportunities. It's not about overnight success; it's about building something sustainable and robust over time.

Is it worth it? Absolutely. Picture this: you've built multiple streams of passive income and you're now free to spend your days exactly how you want. Whether it's traveling, pursuing hobbies, or spending quality time with loved ones, the choice is entirely yours. You don't need to ask for time off or seek permission for a vacation. Your life becomes a canvas, and passive income provides the colors to paint it any way you desire.

In summary, passive income is the ticket to a life unencumbered by financial worries. It converts your dreams into attainable goals, providing the freedom to live life on your terms. The journey to building passive income isn't easy or instantaneous, but the rewards are manifold—financial security, time freedom, and a richer, more fulfilling life. Whether you're at the start of your career or looking for ways to transition out of the rat race, passive income offers a transformative path to true freedom.

So, as we delve into this book, remember that every step you take toward developing passive income streams is a step toward reclaiming your time and achieving the financial freedom to live a life of purpose and passion. Let's begin this journey and explore the endless possibilities that lie ahead.

Chapter 1:
Understanding Passive Income

Diving into passive income is like unlocking a door to more financial freedom and flexibility in your life. It's the money you earn with little to no effort, once the initial setup is complete. Picture this: while you're asleep, enjoying a vacation, or simply binge-watching your favorite TV series, your bank account keeps growing. Passive income can come from various sources such as real estate, dividend stocks, or online businesses. It isn't just about making money, though—understanding the psychology behind it can empower you to think differently about your time and financial strategies. This chapter will demystify the concept, showing you why passive income is a game-changer and setting the stage for exploring the different avenues to generate it effectively.

Types of Passive Income

In our quest to create passive income streams, it's vital to understand the different avenues available. Each type serves as a building block toward the larger goal of financial freedom. You might consider **real estate investments**, which can generate rental income and increase in value over time. *Dividend stocks* offer another route, paying you a portion of a company's earnings without the need to sell your shares. Then there's the realm of **online businesses**, ranging from e-commerce ventures to digital products that sell while you sleep. By diversifying across these types, you reduce risk and pave multiple pathways to earning steady, effort-free income over time.

Real Estate Investments can be one of the most lucrative avenues to develop a robust stream of passive income. It's a classic strategy that has stood the test of time, offering both stability and profitability. When you think about real estate, images of towering skyscrapers or picturesque suburban homes might come to mind. But real estate investment encompasses much more than that. It's about understanding market dynamics, rental yields, property management, and the subtle art of location scouting.

Why is real estate such a powerful instrument in your passive income arsenal? For one, property tends to appreciate over time. While the stock market can be volatile, the value of real estate typically increases, offering potential for capital gains. Moreover, properties can generate consistent rental income, providing a steady cash flow without you having to lift a finger once everything's set up.

One key to successful real estate investing is to focus on the right type of property. Residential properties are often the go-to for beginners. They include single-family homes, duplexes, or apartments. The demand for residential units is almost always strong because people will always need a place to live. You can either rent out your property long-term or opt for short-term rentals like those listed on Airbnb, depending on what suits your financial goals and lifestyle.

However, don't overlook commercial properties, such as office buildings, retail spaces, or multi-family units. While commercial properties can be more complex to manage and require a larger initial investment, they often offer higher rental yields and longer lease periods. Picture owning a small office building rented out to stable businesses—a reliable income source, wouldn't you say?

Let's take a moment to talk about Real Estate Investment Trusts (REITs). If the idea of becoming a landlord doesn't appeal to you or you lack the capital to buy property outright, REITs might be the answer. REITs allow you to invest in real estate without having to deal with the property directly. Think of it as a mutual fund for real estate. You buy shares, and the trust uses the capital to purchase and manage income-generating properties. In return, you get a share of the profits—simple, right?

Location is another critical factor in real estate investment. We've all heard the adage: "Location, location, location." Properties in prime locations tend to appreciate faster and attract higher rents. But what defines a 'prime location'? It's not just about posh neighborhoods. A prime location could be an up-and-coming area ripe for development, offering a balance of affordability and growth potential.

Before taking the plunge, it's crucial to understand the market you're entering. Are you investing in a buyer's market or a seller's market? Is the area's economy growing or stagnant? What are the local vacancy rates? Answering these questions can help you make informed decisions. Extensive market research is non-negotiable. Utilize resources like local real estate reports, online property databases, and even advice from seasoned real estate agents.

Financing your real estate investment is another key consideration. You don't always need to have the entire purchase price in cash. Various financing options are available, from traditional mortgages to private loans. Consider leveraging your money through loans to buy multiple properties, multiplying your potential return. But remember: leverage amplifies both gains and losses, so prudent financial planning is essential.

Handling tenants and property management can either be a hassle or a hands-off experience, depending on how you approach it. If the idea of fixing leaky faucets at midnight terrifies you, hire a property management company. They handle everything—from finding and vetting tenants to maintenance and rent collection. Yes, it will eat into your profits a bit, but considering the stress and time saved, many find it worth the cost.

Tax benefits are another compelling reason to invest in real estate. Rental income isn't subject to self-employment tax, and many expenses incurred in the management and maintenance of the property can be deducted from your taxable income. These may include mortgage interest, property depreciation, maintenance costs, and even certain travel expenses.

But let's keep it real—real estate investments aren't entirely risk-free. Market fluctuations can affect property values, and there can be periods when your property remains vacant, impacting your steady income. Maintenance costs can sometimes come unexpectedly, burning a hole in your pocket. Therefore, having a contingency fund for such unexpected expenses is wise. Earnings won't always be smooth sailing, but with the right planning, it can become a relatively stable part of your passive income strategy.

So, where do you start? It's advisable to begin with thorough education. Read books, take courses, and scout reliable mentors or investment groups. Real-life experience is invaluable, so don't shy away from starting small—perhaps with a single-family home or a modest apartment. As you gain more confidence and understanding, you can gradually scale up your investments.

Lastly, while focusing on the numbers is important, don't forget to consider your personal preferences and lifestyle. Is real estate something you can see yourself managing or being involved in long-term? Does it align with your broader financial goals and life vision? Answering these questions honestly will help ensure that your journey into real estate investment is both profitable and personally satisfying.

Remember, real estate isn't just about buying and selling properties. It's about creating and nurturing assets that work for you, generating income while you sleep. With the right approach, real estate investments can be a cornerstone in your strategy to develop—and sustain—passive income, leading you closer to financial freedom.

Dividend Stocks ...If you are interested in dividends as a part of your passive income strategy, you're not alone. Dividend stocks are a popular choice for many investors looking for a reliable and potentially lucrative income stream. But before we delve into the nitty-gritty, let's lay a little groundwork. What exactly are dividends, and why should you care?

Dividends are essentially a portion of a company's earnings distributed to shareholders. Think of it as a reward for your investment. Companies typically pay dividends quarterly, although the frequency can vary. These payouts can be in the form of cash, additional shares of stock, or other property. The key thing to remember is that not all companies pay dividends. Generally, mature, established companies with steady profits are more likely to offer dividends compared to newer, high-growth companies.

The attraction of dividend stocks lies in their dual potential for income and growth. When you invest in dividend-paying stocks, you benefit not only from the dividends themselves but also from any appreciation in the stock price. It's the best of both worlds, offering you immediate income while allowing your initial investment to grow.

Now, let's break down how to start building a portfolio focused on dividend stocks. First off, it's crucial to do your homework. Research is the name of the game. Look for companies with a history of reliable and growing dividends. The Dividend Aristocrats list is a good place to start. This list includes companies in the S&P 500 that have increased their dividends annually for at least 25 consecutive years. Names like Coca-Cola, Johnson & Johnson, and Procter & Gamble frequently make the cut, given their solid track records.

Income stability is another important factor. You want to make sure that the company has a solid, consistent revenue stream. Check the payout ratio, which is the proportion of earnings a company pays to shareholders as dividends. A payout ratio below 60% is often considered healthy, suggesting the company retains enough earnings to reinvest in itself while still rewarding its shareholders.

Next, consider the yield. Dividend yield is calculated by dividing the annual dividend per share by the stock's current price. It's a handy metric for comparing the income potential of different dividend stocks. However, be cautious of stocks with abnormally high yields. These can sometimes be unsustainable and may signal underlying financial troubles within the company.

Portfolio diversification is key. Don't put all your eggs in one basket. Spread your investments across different sectors to mitigate risk. For instance, consider companies in technology, healthcare, finance, and consumer goods. Diversifying helps to balance the portfolio, ensuring that if one sector underperforms, the others can potentially cushion the blow.

It's also wise to reinvest your dividends, especially in the initial years of your investment journey. Dividend Reinvestment Plans (DRIPs) allow you to automatically reinvest your dividends to buy more shares of the company's stock. This creates a compounding effect, where your initial investment grows exponentially over time. Many brokers and companies offer DRIPs free of charge, which simplifies the process and boosts your returns.

Realize that understanding the tax implications is vital too. Dividends are considered taxable income, and how they're taxed can vary. Qualified dividends are typically taxed at a lower rate compared to ordinary income, whereas non-qualified dividends are taxed at your ordinary income tax rate. Be sure to consult with a tax professional to understand how dividends will impact your tax situation.

Regularly reviewing your portfolio is just as important as the initial selection of stocks. Keep an eye on each company's performance, industry trends, and any shifts in the broader economy that may affect your investments. Don't be afraid to make adjustments when needed. Sometimes, it's necessary to sell underperforming stocks and reinvest the proceeds into better opportunities.

Long-term commitment to a dividend stock strategy can yield significant passive income over time but remember that it's not entirely without risk. Economic downturns, changes in company performance, or shifts in industry dynamics can affect dividend payouts. Therefore, a well-rounded investment strategy that includes other forms of passive income can help mitigate some of these risks. This diversified approach strengthens your financial foundation, giving you multiple streams of income to rely on.

In conclusion, dividend stocks offer an excellent avenue for creating passive income streams. They provide regular cash flow while also offering the potential for capital appreciation. However, success in dividend investing requires careful research, diversified holdings, and an understanding of the tax landscape. By adhering to these principles, you can build a robust dividend stock portfolio that contributes significantly to your financial independence.

Online Businesses have gained unprecedented traction as one of the most feasible ways to develop passive income streams. With less overhead compared to traditional brick-and-mortar businesses, online ventures offer remarkable flexibility and scalability. The best part is, anyone with an internet connection and a handful of tools can start an online business. Whether you're considering launching an e-commerce store, creating digital products, or diving into affiliate marketing, the online world presents endless opportunities to establish recurring revenue streams.

Starting an online business may seem daunting, but the steps to get up and running are simpler than you think. The initial investment can be minimal; often, your time and creativity are your most significant contributions. Many successful online entrepreneurs started as side hustlers, gradually growing their ventures into full-time gigs. The value lies in the scalability—you can start small and expand as you learn and adapt. So, let's break down some of the primary online business models that can serve as passive income sources.

E-commerce has revolutionized the way we shop and do business. Platforms like Shopify, WooCommerce, and BigCommerce have democratized the retail space, enabling individuals to launch their own online stores within hours. Think about dropshipping, where you don't need to worry about inventory or shipping. You source products from suppliers who handle storage and fulfillment, allowing you to focus on marketing and customer service. This model can be particularly appealing if you want to mitigate the risks and initial costs associated with traditional retail businesses.

On the other hand, creating digital products can be incredibly lucrative. Digital products range from ebooks, online courses, and printables, to software and mobile apps. Once created, these products can be sold repeatedly with little additional effort, making them perfect for passive income. Platforms like Udemy, Teachable, and Gumroad provide user-friendly interfaces for creators to monetize their knowledge and skills. The upfront work in development and promotion pays off as you build a library of resources that continue to generate revenue long after they're launched.

Affiliate marketing is yet another powerful strategy. By partnering with brands and companies, you can earn commissions every time someone makes a purchase through your referral link. This model is highly scalable, as you can promote multiple products to a growing audience. Content creators like bloggers, YouTubers, and social media influencers often thrive on affiliate marketing. It's essential to choose products that align with your niche and audience, ensuring authenticity and trust. Successful affiliate marketers are adept at showcasing the value of the products they promote without coming off as overly salesy.

The key to a successful online business lies in automation. Automation tools can handle tasks like email marketing, social media posting, and customer relationship management, allowing you to focus on scaling your business. Services like Mailchimp, Hootsuite, and HubSpot can help streamline these processes, making it easier to manage your operations efficiently. With the right tools, you can turn your online business into a well-oiled machine that operates with minimal manual intervention.

SEO (Search Engine Optimization) is another vital factor that can make or break your online venture. Understanding and implementing SEO practices can drive organic traffic to your site, reducing the need for paid advertising. It's worth investing time in learning about keyword research, on-page optimization, and backlinking strategies. Tools like Google Analytics, SEMrush, and Ahrefs can provide insights into how your site is performing and where improvements can be made. Effective SEO can lead to sustainable, long-term traffic growth and increased revenue.

Online business success also depends on a solid marketing plan. Utilizing multiple channels such as social media, email marketing, and content marketing can amplify your reach. Social media platforms like Facebook, Instagram, and Pinterest are excellent for brand visibility and customer engagement. Email marketing campaigns can nurture leads and retain customers, while content marketing—blogs, podcasts, and videos—can position you as an authority in your niche. A well-rounded marketing strategy ensures that you're not solely reliant on one channel for traffic and sales.

One often overlooked aspect is customer service. In online businesses, exceptional customer service can differentiate you from competitors. Prompt responses to inquiries, transparent communication, and a hassle-free return policy can bolster your reputation and foster customer loyalty. Happy customers are more likely to leave positive reviews and refer your business to others, creating a virtuous cycle of growth.

Of course, running an online business also comes with challenges. Cybersecurity threats and data privacy concerns require constant vigilance. Ensuring your website is secure, using trusted payment gateways, and complying with data protection regulations like GDPR are crucial steps. Investing in good hosting services and regularly updating your software can mitigate many risks.

Moreover, the world of online businesses is highly competitive. Staying ahead requires continuous learning and adaptability. The trends in digital marketing, e-commerce, and consumer behavior are ever-evolving. Keeping an eye on industry news, attending webinars, and participating in online communities can provide valuable insights and opportunities for growth. Networking with other entrepreneurs can also lead to collaborations that can propel your business forward.

One more noteworthy advantage is the global reach. Unlike traditional businesses constrained by location, an online business can attract customers from all corners of the world. This level of accessibility means you can tap into international markets, potentially increasing your sales exponentially. With tools for language translation, global shipping solutions, and international payment processors, expanding your business beyond borders is more manageable than ever before.

Finally, investing in an online business aligns perfectly with the philosophy of passive income. Once the initial setup and optimization are in place, the demand for daily operational involvement greatly diminishes. Of course, the journey requires dedication and smart strategy, but the end result—freedom, both financial and personal—is well worth the effort.

The Psychology of Passive Income

Understanding the nuances of passive income involves more than grasping the technicalities of various income streams. A deep dive into the psychology behind passive income can reveal why some people succeed and others fall short. It transcends simple financial knowledge and dives into mindset, behavioral tendencies, and psychological resilience.

First, let's talk about mindset. Success in generating passive income often begins in the mind. How you perceive money, your capacity for patience, and your willingness to learn can significantly impact your outcomes. Many people are preconditioned to see income as something directly tied to the hours they work. Rewiring this mindset involves understanding that passive income requires upfront efforts and sometimes financial investments that may not pay off immediately. It's about seeing the big picture and trusting the process.

Moreover, building passive income streams can be an emotional roller coaster. It's crucial to prepare for the inevitable highs and lows. The excitement of initial success, the dullness of routine upkeep, and the potential for setbacks or failures require emotional resilience. Individuals who are emotionally prepared for these fluctuations fare better in the long run. It's about not letting short-term failures dictate your long-term plans.

Determining your risk tolerance is another psychological element to consider. Some passive income streams, like dividend stocks or real estate investments, involve varying degrees of risk. Your level of comfort with these risks can influence your choices and, consequently, your success. Understanding your own risk tolerance doesn't just help you choose the right investments; it also prevents you from making impulsive decisions based on fear or greed, which are counterproductive.

In addition, motivation plays a crucial role. Why are you pursuing passive income? Is it to gain financial freedom, retire early, or simply have more time to do what you love? Clarifying your motivation can sustain you through the inevitable rough patches and keep you focused on your goals. An intrinsic motivation, rather than a superficial one, often yields better results because it can carry you through the effort and time required to establish these income streams.

The discipline required to sustain passive income streams is another psychological hurdle. Many types of passive income aren't entirely "set it and forget it." They necessitate regular monitoring, adjustments, and sometimes additional work to optimize returns. Whether it's updating your online business, managing rental properties, or rebalancing your investment portfolio, maintaining discipline is key to long-term success.

Finding the balance between optimism and realism is another psychological balancing act. Overly optimistic individuals might expect quick returns and get discouraged when this doesn't happen. Conversely, overly cautious individuals may never take the necessary risks to get started. The sweet spot is a realistic optimism that recognizes challenges but remains hopeful about overcoming them.

Setting small, achievable milestones can also be psychologically rewarding and can keep you motivated. For instance, instead of aiming to make thousands in the first month, set a goal to establish a solid foundation, like researching the best dividend stocks or purchasing your first real estate investment. These small victories can boost your confidence and encourage you to keep going.

Another critical aspect of the psychology of passive income involves managing external influences and societal pressures. Often, people around you may not understand your goals or may doubt the idea of passive income. Peer pressure can be subtle yet powerful, sometimes making you second-guess your decisions. It's important to surround yourself with like-minded individuals or communities who understand and support your passive income journey.

Financial education also plays a role in the psychological aspect of passive income. Many fears and anxieties related to financial endeavors stem from a lack of knowledge. By educating yourself continuously, you not only increase your practical skills but also your confidence in your ability to make informed decisions. This self-assuredness can be incredibly empowering and can help mitigate the paralysis that often comes with uncertainty.

Lastly, let's talk about the concept of delayed gratification. Passive income often involves a significant amount of delayed gratification. Whether you are investing time, money, or effort, the fruits of your labor may not be immediate. Understanding and accepting this principle can align your expectations and reduce frustration. The ability to delay gratification is often a predictor of success in building passive income.

In summation, the psychology of passive income is a blend of mindset, emotional resilience, risk tolerance, motivation, discipline, and the ability to manage societal pressures. Mastering these psychological aspects can be just as important as understanding the financial principles behind passive income. So, as you embark on your journey to create passive income streams, take the time to train your mind alongside your financial skills. The dual focus will prepare you for the road ahead and increase your chances of long-term success.

Chapter 2:
Setting Your Financial Goals

As you embark on your journey to financial freedom through passive income, it's crucial to set clear financial goals that will guide your decisions and keep you motivated. Start by distinguishing between your short-term and long-term objectives, understanding that each requires different strategies and timeframes. Envision what financial success looks like to you—whether it's achieving a certain level of income, paying off debts, or building a retirement fund—this vision will serve as your north star. Break down these goals into manageable steps, and don't be afraid to adjust them as your circumstances change. By setting well-defined goals, you're not just drifting through the waters of passive income; you're navigating with a purpose, ensuring every move takes you closer to the life you imagine.

Short-Term vs. Long-Term Goals

Before diving headfirst into various ways to develop passive income streams, it's crucial to establish a clear understanding of your short-term and long-term financial goals. Knowing what you want to achieve in both the near future and the distant horizon provides direction, purpose, and a roadmap for your journey. It allows you to align your efforts meaningfully and make informed financial decisions that support your overarching ambitions.

Short-term goals usually cover a period of one to three years. These goals can range from creating an emergency fund to generating a steady side income or paying off high-interest debt. These are the building blocks that stabilize your finances and create a solid foundation for the future. The beauty of short-term goals is that they can provide immediate gratification, enhancing your motivation and keeping you on the right track.

For example, you might set a goal to save $5,000 over the next year. How you achieve this goal could involve cutting down on non-essential expenses, like dining out or subscription services, and reallocating those funds into a high-yield savings account. The progress you make towards this goal can be tracked in real-time, giving you instant feedback and a sense of accomplishment.

On the other hand, long-term goals often extend over a period of five, ten, or even thirty years. Think of these as your financial North Stars—guiding lights that help to navigate through the complexities of life. Long-term goals could include achieving financial independence, buying a home, funding your children's education, or building a retirement nest egg. These are more challenging to attain, requiring sustained effort, patience, and often, a degree of risk-taking.

For these longer-term ambitions, a more diversified and strategic approach is necessary. This could mean investing in dividend-paying stocks, real estate, or building a business that brings in a steady stream of income. While the timelines are longer and the rewards are greater, the path can be fraught with fluctuations and uncertainties. Yet, these goals are critical because they underline your financial legacy and future security.

Striking a balance between short-term and long-term goals is vital. Focusing solely on short-term achievements can make you susceptible to financial complacency, whereas exclusively prioritizing long-term visions could lead to burnout or discouragement. Your financial strategy should be a harmonious blend that includes both immediate rewards and future gains.

One practical way to maintain this balance is by breaking down long-term goals into smaller, more manageable short-term milestones. Let's say one of your long-term goals is to build a portfolio of dividend stocks worth $100,000. You can break this down into annual targets of $10,000 over ten years. This provides you with immediate actionable steps, making a daunting task seem more achievable.

Moreover, it's important to periodically reassess these goals. Life is unpredictable, and circumstances change. Significant life events like marriage, having children, or career shifts might necessitate a reevaluation of your financial aims. Regular check-ins ensure that your goals remain relevant and that your strategies are still aligned with your evolving priorities.

Investing in real estate can serve both short-term and long-term objectives. In the short term, rental income can supplement your current earnings, providing immediate cash flow. Over the long term, property appreciation can significantly boost your net worth. Similarly, dividend stocks offer quarterly payouts now and substantial growth potential over time.

In the realm of online businesses, short-term goals might include launching your first product or generating your initial sales. Over the long term, the vision might be to automate the business to the extent where it runs itself, freeing up your time for other ventures or even further passive income streams. The blend of immediate tasks and future aspirations keeps you engaged and moving forward.

It's not just about the financial metrics; achieving these goals impacts your mental and emotional well-being as well. Short-term wins give you confidence, while long-term planning provides peace of mind. Both play essential roles in your journey to financial freedom.

By setting, balancing, and periodically reviewing your short-term and long-term goals, you'll lay out a financial blueprint that supports your ambition to generate passive income effectively. With this foundation in place, you can move ahead with a clear direction, knowing each step takes you closer to your ultimate financial destiny.

Creating a Vision for Your Life

To set effective financial goals, you first need a clear vision of what you want your life to look like. Crafting a vision means thinking deeply about what truly matters to you, beyond just the numbers in your bank account. Your vision will act as your North Star, guiding you through the ups and downs of your journey to financial independence. It all starts with a dream—a dream that encompasses your personal values, passions, and aspirations.

Start by visualizing your ideal lifestyle. Where do you see yourself living? What kind of house do you dream of having? Perhaps it's a cozy cabin in the mountains or a sleek apartment in the heart of the city. Think about your surroundings and what kind of environment makes you feel most at peace. Picture your daily routine, your work, your hobbies, and the people you want to spend time with.

Once you've painted this mental picture, write it down. Describe your vision in vivid detail as if you are writing a story about your future life. This exercise brings clarity and turns abstract ideas into a concrete plan. Be specific. For example, instead of saying "I want to travel more," say "I want to visit Japan in the spring to see the cherry blossoms."

Now, let's think about your values. What's important to you? Is it freedom, family, adventure, or security? Understanding your core values helps align your financial goals with your life vision. For instance, if family is a top priority, you might focus on creating a passive income stream that allows you to spend more quality time with your loved ones.

Your passions play a significant role in creating your vision, too. What do you love to do? Whether it's painting, writing, cooking, or gardening, weave these passions into your vision. Imagine how you can turn these passions into potential income streams. It makes the journey towards your goals more enjoyable and less of a chore.

Remember that your vision isn't set in stone. Life changes, and so do our dreams and circumstances. Therefore, it's vital to revisit and adjust your vision regularly. This doesn't mean you are being inconsistent; it means you are staying adaptable and open to new opportunities and experiences.

Let's move to another essential component: your long-term aspirations. These are the milestones you want to hit in, say, 10 or 20 years. Do you aspire to retire early? Maybe dream of owning multiple properties, or perhaps you envision yourself as a respected expert in your field. Long-term goals help you plan further into the future, offering a roadmap to follow while leaving room for flexibility.

While long-term vision is crucial, don't overlook the small steps. Short-term goals—like saving for a vacation, paying off debt, or starting a new side hustle—act as stepping stones towards your larger vision. They provide immediate motivation and make the journey more manageable.

Creating a vision for your life also involves financial self-awareness. Take stock of where you currently stand. What are your assets and liabilities? What income streams do you already have, and where are the gaps? Knowing your starting point helps you map out the journey ahead, identifying what you need to focus on to achieve your vision.

It's helpful to create a vision board—a visual representation of your goals and dreams. Collect images, quotes, and any symbols that resonate with your desired future. This board serves as a daily reminder of what you're working towards. Place it somewhere you see often to keep yourself motivated and aligned with your goals.

Another powerful tool is journaling. Reflecting on your journey allows you to process your experiences and track your progress. Write about your successes, challenges, and how you overcame obstacles. This practice not only keeps you focused but also helps you learn from past mistakes and achievements.

One often-overlooked aspect is the emotional component of your vision. Financial goals aren't just about the money—they're about the feelings and experiences that come with achieving those goals. Whether it's the peace of mind from having a secure retirement fund or the thrill of making a successful investment, recognize and embrace these emotions. They are potent motivators.

As you ponder your vision, consider the impact you want to have on the world. How can your financial success contribute to the greater good? Whether it's through philanthropy, volunteering, or supporting causes close to your heart, think about the legacy you wish to leave behind.

Don't forget to involve your family in this vision-creating process. Their support can be invaluable, and ensuring that everyone's dreams align can lead to stronger, more cohesive goal setting. It fosters a sense of unity and shared purpose.

In summary, creating a vision for your life is a multifaceted endeavor that demands introspection, creativity, and planning. It's about blending your dreams with actionable steps, aligning your values with your ambitions, and remaining flexible as life changes. Your vision is the foundation upon which your financial goals will be built, guiding you as you navigate the myriad opportunities and challenges on your way to developing passive income streams and achieving financial freedom.

Chapter 3:
Getting Started with Real Estate

Diving into the world of real estate can seem daunting at first, but it's one of the most reliable pathways to develop a solid passive income stream. To get started, you'll need a foundational understanding of what real estate investment entails, including the types of properties you can invest in, such as residential and commercial properties. It's also important to explore different investment vehicles like Real Estate Investment Trusts (REITs), which allow you to invest in real estate without the need to buy properties outright. By taking the time to learn the basics, understand market conditions, and evaluate potential investments, you'll be on your way to generating a steady income from real estate. The key is research, patience, and being prepared to take calculated risks.

The Basics of Real Estate Investment

Dipping your toes into real estate investment can feel like both an exciting adventure and an intimidating challenge, but it doesn't have to be overwhelming. First and foremost, it's essential to understand the basic principles that will guide you through this journey. Real estate investment primarily involves purchasing properties that will either produce rental income or appreciate in value over time. Whether you're eyeing residential homes, commercial buildings, or multi-family units, the goal is the same: generate a steady cash flow while letting the property's value increase with market trends. You'll be making decisions on location, market conditions, and property management, all of which will shape your success. Understanding these fundamentals will lay a solid foundation for your real estate ventures, setting you up for a profitable experience while contributing to a robust passive income stream.

Residential Properties are often considered the bread and butter of real estate investing. They offer a wealth of opportunities for both new and seasoned investors due to their relative stability and the constant demand for housing. When we talk about residential properties as a source of passive income, we're essentially discussing single-family homes, multi-family units, and occasionally, smaller apartment complexes. The first step in leveraging residential properties to create steady income starts with understanding the types of properties and their respective income potentials.

From cozy bungalows to sprawling estates, residential properties come in all shapes and sizes. Single-family homes are the typical starting point for many investors. They're straightforward to manage, often easier to finance, and can attract long-term tenants. Whether it's a quaint cottage in the suburbs or a posh penthouse in the city, single-family homes can generate consistent rental income with relatively lower management hassles compared to their multi-family counterparts. The simplicity of dealing with a single tenant can't be overstated; fewer disputes, fewer complications, and, generally, less maintenance.

Moving up the ladder, you'll encounter multi-family properties. These are typically duplexes, triplexes, or fourplexes—small buildings with multiple separate living units. The benefit here is evident: multiple income streams from a single property. Imagine owning a triplex: even if one unit is vacant, the other two units can continue to generate income. This provides a buffer against vacancies, making your investment more resilient. Of course, managing multiple tenants can be more complex, but the increase in potential income often makes it worthwhile.

Some investors might find themselves drawn to larger apartment complexes. These can range from a dozen units to a hundred or more. While the potential for income is substantial, so too is the complexity of management. Typically, properties of this size would require professional property management services, but the trade-off is that such investments can yield significant passive income once stabilized. This involves a higher barrier to entry, not just in terms of capital, but in the knowledge and experience needed to manage such a property effectively.

One of the biggest advantages of investing in residential properties is the relative ease of financing. Banks and financial institutions are often more willing to extend mortgages for residential properties due to their predictability and consistent demand. Moreover, residential real estate tends to appreciate over time, adding to the investor's net worth. This appreciation can be leveraged for refinancing, allowing you to extract equity and reinvest in additional properties.

Location, as they say, is everything. Selecting the right area to invest in residential properties can significantly affect your rental income and property value appreciation. Urban areas with growing populations, access to good schools, and amenities like parks and shopping centers have higher rental demands and can command premium rents. That said, investing in up-and-coming neighborhoods can also be lucrative. These areas often have lower entry costs but can experience rapid appreciation as they develop.

Rental strategies play a crucial role in the success of your residential property investments. Long-term rentals are the most common approach, offering stable and predictable income. However, short-term rentals, such as Airbnb, can diversify and potentially maximize income, especially in tourist-heavy areas. That said, short-term rentals often require more active management and can be more susceptible to fluctuations in demand, not to mention varying regulations depending on the location.

The crux of turning your residential properties into a passive income machine lies in the management approach. Self-management can save money but requires a substantial time investment and a knack for dealing with tenant issues, maintenance, and the myriad of small tasks that come with property management. Experienced investors might opt for property management companies to handle these tasks. While this incurs a cost (typically around 10% of the rental income), it frees up your time and can transform your investment into a more passive endeavor.

Tenant selection is another critical aspect. High tenant turnover can erode profits through lost rent and additional make-ready expenses. Conduct thorough background checks, verify income, and check references. Once you have good tenants, keeping them happy with proactive management and timely maintenance can ensure long-term occupancy and reduce vacancies.

Legal and tax implications should also be on your radar when dealing with residential properties. Each state and locality have differing laws regarding landlord-tenant relationships, so familiarize yourself with these to avoid costly legal disputes. Tax-wise, residential investments offer several deductions that can minimize your taxable income. Expenses like mortgage interest, property taxes, insurance, and even the depreciation of the property can be included. Consulting with a real estate-savvy accountant is advisable to fully utilize these benefits.

Finally, it's important to touch on the social impact of investing in residential properties. By providing quality housing, you're not just creating a revenue stream for yourself, but also contributing to your community. Whether it's renovating a neglected property or ensuring your rentals are well-maintained, you're helping improve the neighborhood. This can have a ripple effect, attracting more investments and contributing to overall community development.

In conclusion, residential properties offer a solid foundation for building passive income. From single-family homes to multi-family units and even small apartment complexes, the array of options provide flexibility and scalability. The key lies in strategic property selection, effective management, and an understanding of the market dynamics. Armed with this knowledge, you can confidently step into the world of residential real estate, turning properties into productive, income-generating assets.

Commercial Properties can be the golden goose of passive income. The potential here is massive, but there are also significant challenges. So what exactly makes commercial properties so lucrative? For one, we're talking about spaces leased out to businesses—offices, retail stores, industrial units, and even warehouses. Each of these categories has its unique factors to consider for investment, and the returns can be quite attractive if done right.

One of the primary advantages of investing in commercial properties is the typically higher rental income compared to residential properties. Businesses, especially established ones, are usually willing to pay more for prime locations to attract customers and incentivize employees. Plus, commercial leases often run longer than residential ones—sometimes up to ten years or even more. This kind of stability can make managing and predicting your cash flow a lot easier.

Now, let's dive into location. For commercial properties, location is everything. The proximity to other businesses, the foot traffic, and the accessibility all play a critical role in determining a property's value and potential income. A well-located office building or retail outlet can command high rents and attract quality tenants. However, choosing the right location requires research, possibly more so than residential properties. Look at factors like local economic conditions, future development plans, and the specific needs of the type of business you want to attract.

Leases for commercial properties are generally more complex. You'll deal with terms like Triple Net (NNN) leases, where the tenant is responsible for property taxes, insurance, and maintenance costs. This arrangement can significantly lower your out-of-pocket expenses, but it also means you need to fully understand these lease agreements. You can't afford to be casual about the details here; a well-negotiated lease can save you significant headaches down the line.

Let's talk about the tenants. In commercial properties, business tenants are more likely to take good care of the property because their operations depend on it. The last thing a business wants is to inconvenience its clients due to property issues. Moreover, commercial tenants can sometimes customize the space to fit their business needs, adding value to your property. But remember, having reputable and stable tenants is key. A high turnover of tenants can become a logistical nightmare and eat into your profits.

Diversification is another reason why commercial properties can be a good bet. Mix different types of commercial properties in your portfolio to spread risk. For instance, while an office space might lie vacant during an economic downturn, a warehouse property might still be in high demand due to the rise of e-commerce. This balanced approach can protect your income stream from market fluctuations.

Financing a commercial property is a different ball game compared to residential real estate. Loans for commercial properties typically have shorter terms—think five to ten years—and come with higher interest rates. Lenders will scrutinize your creditworthiness and the property's potential income stream intensely. It's advisable to work with a lender experienced in commercial real estate who can guide you through the process. Also, expect to put down a larger down payment, often around 20-30% of the property value.

Don't forget about property management. Hiring a professional property management firm can be incredibly beneficial. They can handle tenant relations, maintenance issues, and day-to-day operations, freeing you up to concentrate on growing your portfolio or enjoying your passive income. While this will cut into your profits, the peace of mind and saved time can be well worth the expense. Make sure to choose a management company with a solid track record and good reviews from other property owners.

Pitfalls exist, as they do with any investment. Market fluctuations can impact rental income and property values. Unlike residential properties, commercial spaces might remain vacant for longer periods, which can strain your finances. It's crucial to have a financial cushion to cover the mortgage and other operating expenses during these times. Developing a solid financial and risk management strategy can help mitigate these risks.

Legal considerations also play a significant role. Zoning laws, accessibility requirements (like ADA compliance in the United States), and environmental regulations can all affect your property's suitability for certain types of businesses. Consulting with a real estate attorney can help you navigate these complexities and avoid costly mistakes.

The tax benefits of commercial real estate investment can't be overlooked either. From mortgage interest deductions to depreciation, there are various ways to lower your tax burden. However, commercial real estate rules are intricate, so it's a good idea to have a tax advisor who specializes in real estate to guide you through the process.

Technology is revolutionizing the way we invest in and manage commercial properties. Platforms like CoStar provide detailed market analytics, while software solutions offer end-to-end property management tools that can make your life a whole lot easier. Make sure to leverage these technologies to stay ahead of the curve and make informed decisions.

Lastly, consider long-term trends that could impact commercial real estate, such as the shift towards remote work. Office spaces might see a decline in demand, while logistics and industrial spaces could grow due to the rise of online shopping. Keeping an eye on these trends will allow you to adjust your strategy accordingly and stay profitable.

By strategically investing in commercial properties, you can achieve a sustainable and lucrative passive income stream. From understanding lease agreements and financing options to navigating legal requirements and market trends, the path may be complex, but the rewards can be significant. With careful planning and smart management, commercial properties can become a cornerstone of your passive income portfolio.

Real Estate Investment Trusts (REITs)

Real Estate Investment Trusts (REITs) offer a splendid avenue for those interested in real estate investments but lack the capital to buy properties directly. With REITs, you can invest in real estate without purchasing actual properties, gaining exposure to real estate markets in a way that's far more accessible—financially and logistically—for most investors. Essentially, REITs are companies that own, operate, or finance income-generating real estate. These companies pool funds from multiple investors to acquire and manage a portfolio of properties or real estate loans.

One of the most striking advantages of REITs is liquidity. Unlike owning real estate properties, which can take months or even years to sell, REIT shares can be traded on the stock market similarly to other stocks. This gives investors the flexibility to enter and exit positions more freely. Imagine being able to dip into property investments and liquidate them at your convenience—REITs make this possible.

There are different types of REITs you can choose from, each offering unique benefits and risks. Equity REITs, for example, own and manage real estate properties. They generate revenue primarily through leasing spaces and collecting rents on the properties they own. This type can be a steady income generator due to the regular rent payments. On the other hand, Mortgage REITs (mREITs) offer a slightly different flavor by focusing on real estate loans and earning income from interest. They can come with different risk profiles but offer higher yields compared to equity REITs.

Publicly traded REITs are listed on major stock exchanges, making them easily accessible for everyone. These REITs must adhere to certain regulations which add a layer of protection for investors. On the flip side, there are also non-publicly traded REITs, which might be available but come with their own set of complexities and often are less liquid. If you are seeking transparency and ease of trade, publicly traded REITs are a more suitable option.

Now, let's talk about dividends. REITs are known for their attractive dividend payouts. By law, REITs must distribute at least 90% of their taxable income to shareholders in the form of dividends. This can provide a consistent and predictable income stream for investors, which is one of the key components when you're looking to build passive income streams. Imagine setting up an account that sends you regular payouts while you're off spending time on things you genuinely love—that's the beauty of REITs.

Diversification is another compelling benefit. Investing in REITs allows you to spread your investment across various real estate sectors, be it residential, commercial, or industrial. This way, you're not putting all your eggs in one basket. For instance, if the residential market takes a hit, commercial properties in your REIT portfolio might still perform well, thereby balancing your returns. This diversification can help hedge against market volatility, offering a more stable investment experience.

Furthermore, getting started with REITs is straightforward. You can begin investing with a relatively small amount of money. There's no need to deal with property management headaches or finding tenants. The professional management teams running REITs handle everything, letting you enjoy the income without the operational stress. Also, with the prevalence of online brokerage platforms, purchasing REIT shares can be done in just a few clicks.

REITs also offer tax advantages. Though dividends from REITs are generally taxed as ordinary income, other tax benefits may apply depending on your situation and the specific REIT. Always consult a tax advisor to understand how REIT investments fit into your broader tax strategy.

Understanding the risks involved is equally important. REITs are subject to market risks and factors like interest rate fluctuations, property market dynamics, and economic conditions. For instance, rising interest rates can affect REIT stock prices since borrowing costs for the REITs increase, potentially squeezing profit margins. Be mindful and stay informed about these variables to make well-rounded investment decisions.

Now, if you're wondering how to pick the right REITs to invest in, due diligence is key. Investigate the management team's expertise, the performance track record, and the portfolio's composition. Look for REITs with a solid history of dividend payments, a diversified portfolio, and strong governance structures. Financial metrics like Funds from Operations (FFO) can offer insights into the REIT's profitability, providing a clue about future dividend prospects.

It's worth noting that starting with a REIT ETF (Exchange-Traded Fund) can be a smart move for beginners. REIT ETFs invest in a diversified basket of REITs, offering exposure to multiple real estate markets and reducing the risk associated with any single REIT. This approach lets you benefit from broader market trends and reduces the complexity involved in selecting individual REITs.

Education is your best ally here. Take the time to learn about different REIT sectors—residential, healthcare, industrial, retail, and more. Each has its unique market drivers and risk factors. For example, healthcare REITs might thrive in an aging population scenario, while retail REITs might struggle with the rise of e-commerce. Understanding these dynamics will help you make better-informed decisions.

Another significant aspect is performance monitoring. Regularly review your REITs' performance against your financial goals. Is the dividend yield meeting your income expectations? Are the underlying properties appreciating in value, or is there a concerning vacancy rate? Keeping an eye on these factors will help you stay on track and adjust your strategy when necessary.

Lastly, don't forget the human element—networking with other investors. Join forums, attend real estate investment clubs, or take part in webinars and conferences. Sharing experiences and strategies can provide invaluable insights and might reveal opportunities you hadn't considered. Building a community around your investment journey can provide both support and fresh perspectives.

In summary, REITs can be a powerful tool in your passive income arsenal. They offer the allure of real estate investment without the capital and management burden of owning properties yourself. With their attractive dividends, diversification benefits, and high liquidity, REITs can help you step closer to achieving financial freedom. Like any investment, they come with their risks and require thoughtful consideration, but with the right approach, REITs can be a fantastic addition to your passive income portfolio.

Investing in REITs isn't just about growing your wealth; it's about buying back your time and inching toward the life you've always dreamed of. Whether you're a seasoned investor or a complete beginner, REITs provide a practical, engaging, and potentially very rewarding way to make your money work for you.

Chapter 4:
Investing in the Stock Market

Diving into the stock market might seem like decoding an enigma wrapped in a riddle, but it's one of the most accessible methods to build a passive income stream. With a bit of knowledge and patience, you can turn your hard-earned money into a steady flow of dividends and capital gains. The key is understanding how to evaluate stocks, knowing when to buy and sell, and diversifying your investments to mitigate risks. By building a well-rounded dividend stock portfolio, you're not just investing in companies; you're investing in your future financial freedom. So, take a deep breath, start small, and let the power of compounding work its magic over time. The stock market might have its highs and lows, but with a strategic approach, it can be a treasure trove of opportunity.

Understanding Dividends

So, you're diving into the exciting world of the stock market, huh? Well, understanding dividends is a fantastic place to start. Dividends, in simple terms, are payments made by a corporation to its shareholders. When a company earns a profit, it has several options: reinvest those profits into the business, pay down debt, or distribute some of them to you – the shareholder – in the form of dividends. Think of dividends as the company's way of saying, "Thanks for sticking with us."

Now, let's break it down further. Not all companies pay dividends. Typically, firms that are well-established and financially sound—think major players like Coca-Cola or Procter & Gamble—tend to offer regular dividend payouts. These companies are often referred to as "blue-chip" stocks. By investing in such dividend-paying stocks, you can create a steady stream of passive income as long as you hold onto the shares. And let's face it, who doesn't like the idea of getting paid just for owning something?

Dividends can come in various forms. The most common type is cash dividends, where the payment is made directly to your brokerage account. Some companies, however, might offer stock dividends. Instead of cash, these firms give you additional shares of stock. While not money in your pocket immediately, stock dividends can still boost your portfolio's value over time. Either way, understanding these options will help you make informed decisions based on your financial goals.

The amount of the dividend payment is usually expressed as a dollar amount per share or a percentage of the stock's current price, known as the dividend yield. For example, if a company declares a $1 dividend per share and you own 100 shares, you'd receive $100. The dividend yield, on the other hand, is calculated by dividing the annual dividend by the stock's current price. So if our hypothetical stock were trading at $50, the yield would be 2% ($1/$50). Higher yields might seem attractive, but they can also signal higher risk, so it's essential to do your homework.

Investing in dividend-paying stocks isn't just about the payouts; it's also about the stability they often represent. Companies that consistently pay and grow their dividends are usually financially healthy and well-managed. Dividend growth—when a company raises its dividend over time—can be a signal of a strong business model and robust cash flow. This consistent growth can provide you with a hedge against inflation, building your passive income stream in real terms, year after year.

During tougher economic times, dividends can provide a cushion. While stock prices may fluctuate wildly, companies with solid dividend histories may keep their payouts steady, giving you a reliable income stream. However, it's crucial to note that dividends aren't guaranteed. Companies can cut or eliminate their dividend if they encounter financial trouble. Hence, diversifying your portfolio to include various sectors can mitigate some of this risk.

One powerful strategy for building wealth through dividends is dividend reinvestment plans, commonly known as DRIPs. Instead of taking your dividend in cash, you can reinvest it to purchase more shares of the stock. Over time, the compounding effect—reinvesting your earnings to generate even more earnings—can substantially grow your investment. Many brokerage firms offer this service at no additional cost, making it an easy way to boost your portfolio's growth.

Investing in dividend-paying stocks can be an excellent strategy for those looking for regular income, but balancing it within your larger investment strategy is critical. Make sure to diversify your investments to manage risk effectively. Overcommitting to high-yield dividend stocks might expose you to more volatility than you're prepared to handle.

Let's talk about taxes for a moment. Yes, Uncle Sam will want a piece of your dividend pie. In the U.S., dividends are generally taxed as either ordinary income or qualified dividends. Ordinary dividends are taxed at your regular income tax rate, while qualified dividends benefit from the lower long-term capital gains tax rates. Most dividends from U.S. companies qualify, but it's essential to read up on the specifics to understand your tax obligations. Consulting with a tax advisor can save you a headache and help you optimize your investment strategy.

Some investors specifically look for companies known as "dividend aristocrats." These are firms that have increased their dividends annually for at least 25 consecutive years. These stocks are often more stable and can offer both income and growth potential. Companies like Johnson & Johnson and 3M typically fall into this category. They offer a compelling mix of reliability and the potential for long-term growth in both stock price and dividend payouts.

To sum it up, understanding dividends is not just about knowing you'll get a check every quarter. It's about grasping how these payments can fit into your overall investment strategy to help you achieve your financial goals. Dividends can offer a dependable income stream, potential tax advantages, and a signal of a company's financial health. By focusing on companies with a history of steady or growing dividend payouts, you can set yourself up for a stable, passive income that supports your journey toward financial freedom.

Are dividends the be-all and end-all of stock market investing? Not quite. They're one piece of a much larger puzzle. But for those seeking passive income, they can offer a reliable and rewarding path. Keep learning, stay diversified, and remember that consistency and informed decision-making are your best allies in the stock market arena.

Building a Dividend Stock Portfolio

Investing in the stock market can seem like an overwhelming venture, but building a dividend stock portfolio is a compelling strategy for those looking to generate passive income. It doesn't just provide the potential for capital gains; it also offers a steady stream of income through dividends, which are earnings shared with shareholders regularly. Unlike other investments, dividend stocks can be a more stable source of income, especially when talking about blue-chip companies with a long history of dividend payments.

Understanding the basics is crucial: dividends are essentially a portion of a company's profit distributed to shareholders. The amount can vary based on the company's performance and policies. Some companies pay quarterly, while others might opt for an annual distribution. The relative predictability of dividends can make them an attractive choice for those looking to fund their retirement or achieve financial independence.

The first step in building a dividend stock portfolio is research. You must identify companies that consistently pay dividends and have a solid history of financial performance. Start by looking at industry leaders known for their stable earnings and dividend growth. Companies in sectors like utilities, consumer goods, and healthcare often make good candidates because they generally maintain steady revenue, even in economic downturns.

Consider stock selection criteria carefully. A good dividend stock usually has a dividend yield between 2% and 6%. A higher yield might seem attractive but can sometimes indicate underlying issues with the company. Another metric worth considering is the payout ratio, which shows the proportion of earnings paid out as dividends. A sustainable payout ratio usually falls between 40% to 60%, ensuring the company retains enough earnings for future growth and emergencies.

Once you've identified suitable stocks, it's time to diversify. Diversification mitigates risk. Allocating your investments across multiple industries can protect you from significant losses if one sector underperforms. Aim to have at least 10 to 15 different dividend-paying stocks across various sectors. This spread helps balance the portfolio, making it more resilient against market volatility.

Next comes the essential step of regular portfolio maintenance. Simply buying dividend stocks and forgetting about them isn't enough. Regularly reviewing your portfolio ensures that the stocks you picked are still good candidates for long-term investments. Keep an eye on their earnings reports, dividend announcements, and any significant news that could impact their performance. Reevaluate your investments periodically and be prepared to adjust as necessary to maintain or improve the overall health of your portfolio.

Reinvesting dividends can further amplify your returns. Many brokerage firms offer dividend reinvestment plans (DRIPs), allowing you to automatically reinvest your dividend payouts into more shares of the same stock. This reinvestment compounds your returns over time, increasing both your stock holdings and potential future dividends. It's a powerful tool for growing your portfolio without additional cash investments.

Another aspect to consider is tax implications. Dividends are usually subject to taxes, and these can eat into your returns if you're not careful. Depending on the type of account you hold, dividends can be taxed as ordinary income or at the qualified dividend rate, which is typically lower. Strategies like holding dividend-paying stocks in tax-advantaged accounts (such as IRAs) can mitigate the tax burden and maximize your returns.

Now, navigating the ever-shifting landscape of the stock market requires staying informed. Various online platforms and financial publications can offer insights and alerts about your investments. Subscription services, news websites, and even mobile apps can provide timely updates on stock performance. Developing the habit of continual learning keeps you positioned to make informed decisions and adapt to market changes swiftly.

Consider using a brokerage firm or financial advisor if you're not confident managing your portfolio. While DIY investing can be empowering and cost-effective, professional advice can offer personalized strategies that align with your financial goals and risk tolerance. Advisors can provide valuable insights, especially when it comes to complex tax situations and estate planning, ensuring your investments align with your broader financial picture.

Sometimes, you may encounter company stock splits or changes in dividend policies. A stock split increases the number of shares, reducing the price per share but retaining the total market value of your holdings. In contrast, if a company cuts its dividend, it may indicate financial trouble, potentially prompting you to reassess whether it remains a good fit for your portfolio. Being vigilant about these changes helps maintain a balanced and healthy portfolio.

Innovation in financial technology has made building and managing a dividend stock portfolio more accessible than ever before. Robo-advisors, automated investment platforms, allow you to set preferences and risk levels while they manage your investments based on algorithms. These platforms often feature lower fees compared to traditional advisors and can be an excellent option for those just starting.

Remember, patience is your ally in dividend investing. Building a portfolio that provides a reliable income stream takes time and persistence. Don't be swayed by short-term market fluctuations. Instead, focus on the long-term growth potential and consistent income generation. A well-constructed dividend stock portfolio can significantly contribute to your financial freedom, enabling you to enjoy the peace of mind that comes with a stable and predictable income stream.

In summary, building a dividend stock portfolio involves diligent research, careful selection, regular maintenance, and diversification. It's not a get-rich-quick scheme but a steady and reliable way to grow your wealth over time. Combining the analytical rigor of selecting strong dividend-paying companies with the benefits of reinvesting dividends and managing taxes efficiently positions you to build a solid passive income stream. Investing in dividend stocks can pave the way to financial freedom, providing you with the means to enjoy life on your terms.

Chapter 5:
The Online Entrepreneur

What's more exhilarating than the idea of making money while you sleep? Welcome to the world of the online entrepreneur, where the possibilities are only limited by your creativity and drive. Whether you're dreaming of running a thriving e-commerce store, selling your own digital products, or capitalizing on affiliate marketing, the online space offers multiple avenues to create sustainable passive income streams. It all starts with identifying a niche that resonates with you, then strategically building and marketing your presence. Harness the power of social media, email lists, and SEO to drive traffic and convert visitors into loyal customers. This chapter will not only guide you through the fundamentals but also offer practical tips and resources to set you on the path to online entrepreneurial success.

Starting an E-Commerce Business

Starting an e-commerce business can seem like a daunting task, especially if you're diving into it for the first time. However, when done right, it can become a lucrative and relatively passive income stream. The digital marketplace has leveled the playing field, allowing even small players to compete with larger businesses. With a bit of knowledge and a clear plan, you'll find yourself well on your way to creating a profitable online venture.

Before we dive into the nitty-gritty, let's clarify what an e-commerce business actually is. At its core, e-commerce involves selling goods or services online. This could be through your own website, third-party marketplaces like Amazon or eBay, or social media platforms. The beauty of e-commerce lies in its flexibility. You can start small and scale your operations as your business grows.

The first crucial step in starting an e-commerce business is choosing the right product or service to sell. This decision can make or break your venture, so you'll want to put considerable thought into it. Begin by conducting market research to identify gaps in the market and current buying trends. What problems are people facing that you could solve? Look at competitors and study their strengths and weaknesses. Your goal is to find a unique value proposition that sets you apart.

After identifying a promising product or service, validating your idea is essential. You can test the waters by creating a minimal viable product (MVP) and gathering feedback from a small audience. Launch a basic version of your product and closely monitor how it's received. This not only helps in refining your offering but also minimizes risk by ensuring there's demand before committing significant resources.

Once you're confident in your product, you'll need to choose a business model. There are several to consider, each with its advantages and disadvantages. The most common models include:

- **Business-to-Consumer (B2C):** Selling directly to individual consumers.

- **Business-to-Business (B2B):** Selling to other businesses, often in bulk.

- **Consumer-to-Consumer (C2C):** Facilitating sales between consumers, like on eBay.

- **Subscription Model:** Offering products or services on a recurring basis.

Your choice of platform can significantly influence the success of your e-commerce business. For instance, building your own website using a platform like Shopify, Magento, or WooCommerce offers control and flexibility but comes with a learning curve. Alternatively, you can opt for established marketplaces like Amazon, which provide an existing customer base but charge fees and limit branding opportunities.

Branding is another critical aspect that you shouldn't overlook. Your brand encompasses more than just your logo and company name; it's the overall perception people have of your business. A strong brand builds trust and loyalty, making it easier to attract and retain customers. Invest in a professional logo, create a consistent color scheme, and develop a unique brand voice that resonates with your target audience.

Next up is the website's design and user experience. In e-commerce, first impressions matter immensely. A well-designed, user-friendly website can significantly boost your conversion rates. Focus on creating a clean layout, easy navigation, and fast loading times. Also, don't neglect mobile optimization, as a large portion of online shopping occurs on mobile devices.

You've set up your online store; now it's time to drive traffic to it. Effective digital marketing strategies are crucial for attracting visitors and converting them into customers. Utilize a mix of search engine optimization (SEO), pay-per-click (PPC) advertising, social media marketing, and email campaigns. Each of these channels has its dynamics, so you'll need to tailor your approach to suit your specific goals and audience.

SEO plays a pivotal role in getting your online store noticed. By optimizing your site for search engines, you increase its visibility to potential customers. Conduct keyword research to identify terms that your target audience uses when searching for products like yours.

Incorporate these keywords into your product descriptions, blog posts, and meta tags to improve your search engine rankings.

Social media marketing is equally important for e-commerce businesses. Platforms like Facebook, Instagram, and Pinterest are invaluable tools for reaching potential customers and building relationships with them. Share engaging content, run targeted ads, and interact with your audience to build a loyal following. Consider partnering with influencers who can promote your products to their followers, amplifying your reach.

One thing many new entrepreneurs overlook is the importance of customer service. Exceptional customer service can set you apart from competitors and create a loyal customer base. Make it easy for customers to contact you, whether through live chat, email, or phone. Respond promptly and courteously to inquiries and resolve any issues swiftly. Happy customers are more likely to leave positive reviews and recommend your business to others.

As your e-commerce business grows, you'll need to think about scalability. Automating routine tasks can free up your time and ensure smoother operations. Tools for inventory management, order fulfillment, and customer relationship management can streamline your processes and help you handle increased demand. Investing in these tools early on can save you a lot of headaches down the road.

Payment processing is another area that requires careful consideration. Offering a variety of payment options can improve the user experience and reduce cart abandonment rates. Most e-commerce platforms integrate with popular payment gateways like PayPal, Stripe, and Square, making it easier to accommodate customers' preferences.

Shipping and fulfillment are critical aspects that directly impact customer satisfaction. Clear policies and reliable logistics partners can help ensure that orders are delivered on time and in good condition.

Consider offering multiple shipping options, including express delivery, to cater to different customer needs. Providing tracking information can further enhance the customer experience by keeping them informed every step of the way.

Return policies are another important element. A fair and transparent return policy can build trust and encourage purchases. Make sure your policy is easy to understand and prominently displayed on your website. Clearly outline the steps for returns and exchanges, and ensure your customer service team is well-equipped to handle these requests professionally and efficiently.

Finally, keep an eye on your metrics to evaluate your e-commerce business's performance. Tools like Google Analytics can provide insights into your site's traffic, user behavior, and sales. Key performance indicators (KPIs) such as conversion rates, average order value, and customer lifetime value can help you identify areas for improvement and make data-driven decisions.

In conclusion, starting an e-commerce business involves various steps, from choosing the right product and business model to creating a user-friendly website and implementing effective marketing strategies. While it may seem overwhelming, each element is an essential piece of the puzzle that contributes to your venture's overall success. With careful planning, continuous learning, and a customer-centric approach, you'll be well on your way to building a thriving e-commerce business that serves as a robust source of passive income.

Creating Digital Products

When it comes to building a sustainable online business, few avenues are as lucrative as creating digital products. Tailored to be sold online, these products refer to any commodities that people can purchase, download, and use digitally. Think eBooks, online courses, software applications, and graphic design templates, just to name a few. The appeal of digital products lies in their scalability—once created, they can be sold an infinite number of times with virtually no overhead costs. Let's delve into the various types of digital products you could create and the essential steps to building them.

First and foremost, consider starting with the low-hanging fruit: eBooks. If you've got knowledge in a specific field, creating an eBook can be an excellent way to share your expertise while generating income. What's great about eBooks is that the barrier to entry is fairly low. You don't need to be a seasoned author; as long as you can articulate your thoughts clearly and offer valuable, actionable content, you're good to go. Don't forget about proper formatting and design. Tools like Microsoft Word or design software like Adobe InDesign can be invaluable here.

Then there's the world of online courses. With sites like Udemy, Teachable, and Coursera revolutionizing education, there's a massive demand for specialized knowledge that people can learn at their own pace. If you're an expert in anything—coding, culinary arts, or even personal finance—you can create modules, record video lectures, and bundle them into a course. It requires a bit more work upfront compared to eBooks, but the return on investment can be significantly higher. Imagine hundreds, if not thousands, of people purchasing your course while you're off spending quality time with loved ones or even working on your next big project.

Software as a digital product is another dynamic area where there's seemingly endless potential. Whether it's a productivity app, a game, or a useful tool like a budgeting calculator, software products can range from simple to complex. Building software usually requires some coding skills, but don't be discouraged if programming isn't your forte. Platforms like Appy Pie and Bubble make it possible to create apps without intricate coding knowledge. Also, consider hiring freelance developers if your project demands a more complex skill set. This investment can pay off substantially, given the high value customers place on functional, user-friendly software.

Templates and graphic designs are other lucrative digital products. Websites, presentations, social media posts, and resumes—all of these can benefit from well-designed templates. If you have a keen eye for aesthetics and proficiency in tools like Adobe Illustrator, Photoshop, or even Canva, you could create and sell templates that considerably enhance users' work quality and efficiency. Marketplaces like Etsy and Creative Market make it easy to reach a broad audience eager for high-quality designs.

That said, creating digital products isn't just about the product itself; the planning and research phases are crucial. Start by understanding your target audience. What problems do they face, and how can your digital product solve them? Market research tools like Google Trends, forums, and social media can offer invaluable insights. Validation is also essential. Before sinking time and resources into creating a product, consider pre-selling or conducting surveys to ensure there's a demand.

Once you've got a clear picture of what you intend to create, outline a production plan. Break the project into manageable stages and set deadlines for each phase to keep yourself on track. Let's say you're creating an online course. Your plan could include research, outlining the syllabus, creating video content, editing, and finally, marketing.

In terms of tools, there's no shortage of options to help streamline the creation process. For eBooks, Scrivener and Adobe InDesign are popular choices. For online courses, think about investing in a good microphone and video editing software like Camtasia or Adobe Premiere Pro. Software developers might leverage platforms like

Github or Visual Studio Code. And graphic designers will find familiar tools in Adobe Creative Cloud or Canva.

Creating a digital product also necessitates a good deal of testing. Especially for software and online courses, beta testing can help you identify issues and areas for improvement. Engage a small group of users to try out your product and provide feedback. This can be a game-changer in delivering a polished final product that meets or exceeds user expectations.

Marketing your digital product is equally important and deserving of its chapter, but it's worth touching on briefly here. Leverage your existing network for initial launches and beta testing. Social media platforms—Twitter, Instagram, LinkedIn—can help you reach a larger audience. Email marketing is another robust option; build a mailing list of potential customers who have shown interest in your product niche.

It's also worth noting the power of collaborations and partnerships. Pairing up with influencers or other experts in your field can give your product significant exposure. Consider affiliate programs where others can earn a commission for selling your product, thereby expanding your reach without additional marketing expenses. These strategies often result in a win-win situation, amplifying your marketing efforts far more than you could solo.

Monetizing your digital product might require some creativity. Depending on what you're offering, you could pursue several different pricing models. eBooks typically use a one-time purchase model, whereas software can adopt a subscription-based model for ongoing revenue. Online courses might offer tiered pricing based on the content's depth and level of access.

Don't hesitate to bundle products. If you've got an eBook and an online course on related topics, why not offer them together at a discounted price? This not only increases the perceived value but often leads to higher sales volumes. Limited-time offers and discounts can create a sense of urgency, prompting quick decisions from potential buyers. Offering free resources like sample chapters or trial periods can also act as a hook to entice customers into purchasing the full product.

Another important aspect is managing customer feedback and adapting. The digital world evolves quickly, and staying ahead means continuously improving your product. Set up mechanisms to collect feedback, such as surveys or reviews, and be responsive. Updates and new versions can keep the product fresh and meet customer expectations. This kind of adaptability often translates to greater customer loyalty and newfound credibility.

Digital products offer a rewarding path to creating passive income streams. They demand upfront effort, particularly in the creation and marketing phases, but the rewards can be substantial and long-lasting. By leveraging your unique skills and tapping into emerging trends, you can carve out a niche in the ever-expanding digital marketplace. So, get started today—your future self will thank you.

Affiliate Marketing

Affiliate marketing is like being a digital middleman, but instead of dealing with physical goods in a market, you're connecting people with products and services online. It's a powerful method for generating passive income, primarily because it requires little to no upfront investment. You don't need to buy stock, manage shipping, or deal with customer service. Essentially, you're earning commissions by promoting someone else's products or services. Quite appealing, right?

There's a bit of magic behind effective affiliate marketing – a mix of understanding your audience, picking the right products, and employing strategic techniques to drive traffic. Let's dive into how you can become a savvy affiliate marketer and start seeing those commissions roll in.

First and foremost, selecting the right niche is critical. When you specialize or focus on a particular market segment, you position yourself as an expert, making your recommendations and content more credible. Think about areas you are passionate about or have in-depth knowledge of. This could range from fitness and health products to tech gadgets, financial advice, or even pet supplies. Remember, the more specific your niche, the better. For instance, instead of targeting general fitness enthusiasts, you could focus on vegan bodybuilding.

After choosing your niche, you'll need to identify suitable affiliate programs. There are countless affiliate networks like Amazon Associates, ClickBank, and Commission Junction. These platforms connect publishers (that's you) with merchants offering products or services. When exploring affiliate programs, examine the commission rates, cookie duration (how long your referral will earn you a commission), and payout methods. Opt for programs that align with your niche and offer generous commissions.

Creating quality content is another pillar of successful affiliate marketing. Whether it's blog posts, YouTube videos, or social media updates, your content should provide value, educate, and engage your audience. It's not enough to just slap affiliate links everywhere. You must weave them into your content strategically and naturally. Write product reviews, make tutorial videos, or create listicles that recommend top products in your niche. And don't forget SEO – quality content needs to be discoverable!

Building a loyal audience takes time and consistency. Engage with your audience through various channels. Start a blog or a YouTube channel, and regularly post content related to your niche. Use email marketing to keep your audience updated on new content, promotions, or special deals. Encourage interaction by asking questions, conducting polls, or hosting live sessions. The more engaged your audience is, the more likely they are to trust your recommendations.

Traffic is the lifeblood of affiliate marketing. To drive traffic to your content, you'll need to diversify your approach. Social media platforms like Facebook, Instagram, and Pinterest can be goldmines if used correctly. Paid advertising through Google AdWords or Facebook Ads can also generate traffic quickly if you have the budget. Collaborate with influencers in your niche for guest posts or joint projects to tap into their audience. Diversification ensures that you're not overly reliant on a single source of traffic.

Monitoring and analyzing your efforts is crucial. Use tools like Google Analytics or the analytics provided by your affiliate networks to track clicks, conversions, and earnings. Analyze which types of content and promotional strategies are most effective. This data allows you to refine your strategies, boost your performance, and ultimately increase your commissions. Successful affiliate marketers continuously tweak and optimize their approaches.

Let's not forget about trust and transparency. Disclose your affiliate relationships to your audience. Honesty builds trust, and audiences appreciate it when you're upfront about how you make money. This doesn't mean you need to shout it from the rooftops. A simple disclaimer at the beginning or end of your content suffices. When people sense authenticity, they're more inclined to follow your recommendations and click those all-important affiliate links.

Affiliate marketing also involves keeping abreast with trends and adapting to changes. Technologies, platforms, and consumer behaviors evolve, affecting how you should approach your marketing strategies. Subscribe to industry news, follow leading affiliate marketers, and join forums or communities to stay updated. Being proactive in learning and adapting keeps you ahead of the game and maximizes your passive income potential.

Lastly, don't overlook the power of building relationships. Forming connections with other affiliate marketers, product owners, and even your audience opens up opportunities for collaboration, mentorship, and mutual growth. Join affiliate marketing groups or attend industry conferences to network and share experiences.

In summary, affiliate marketing, while a powerful passive income strategy, requires thoughtful planning, strategic execution, and continuous learning. By choosing the right niche, partnering with quality affiliate programs, creating compelling content, driving traffic, being transparent, analyzing performance, staying updated, and building relationships, you can carve a niche for yourself in the world of affiliate marketing. The road might be bumpy at first, but persistence and perseverance will pave your way to a steady stream of passive income.

Chapter 6:
Building a Blog that Earns

So you've decided you want a blog that doesn't just share your thoughts but lines your pockets too. Let's dive into the nuts and bolts of building a blog that earns. First, finding your niche is like picking your character in a game—this decision will shape your entire strategy. You want to target a topic you're passionate about and that has an audience willing to engage. Next, we're talking content creation and SEO, the bread and butter of your blog. Crafting high-quality posts peppered with strategic keywords will not only draw readers but also keep search engines happy. Lastly, monetizing your blog is where things get interesting; think affiliate links, sponsored posts, and even selling your own products or services. Each method has its quirks, but together they'll transform your blog from just another site into a revenue-generating machine.

Finding Your Niche

So, you've decided to start a blog to earn passive income. It's an exciting journey, but before you dive into creating content, the first crucial step is finding your niche. This isn't something you should rush. Choosing the right niche is the bedrock upon which your entire blogging journey will be built.

Finding your niche is all about identifying a specific topic you're passionate about and one that has the potential to attract and engage an audience. The perfect niche strikes a balance between something you love and something others want to read about. Why? Because when you're genuinely interested in a topic, your enthusiasm will shine through in your writing. And it's this authenticity that will draw readers in and keep them coming back for more.

First, think about your interests and expertise. What are the subjects that you could talk about for hours without getting bored? Maybe it's travel, technology, personal finance, or even vegan cooking. Jot down a list of potential topics. Don't censor yourself at this point; just let the ideas flow. The more, the better.

Once you've compiled your list, it's time to evaluate the market demand for each topic. A simple way to do this is by using keyword research tools like Google Keyword Planner or Ahrefs. These tools will show you how often people search for terms related to your potential niche topics. You're looking for a sweet spot—topics that have a decent search volume but aren't overly saturated with competition.

Another aspect to consider is your target audience. Who are the people you want to reach with your blog? Are they millennials, parents, entrepreneurs, or maybe fitness enthusiasts? Understanding your audience helps you create targeted content that resonates with them. It's also wise to check out forums, social media groups, and other blogs in your prospective niche. Observe what kind of questions people are asking and what types of content are getting the most engagement.

Let's take a moment to talk about profitability. Not all niches are created equal when it comes to earning potential. Some topics might be popular, but they might not offer many opportunities for monetization. For instance, a blog about luxury travel can attract high-paying advertisers and sponsorships, whereas a blog about poetry might struggle to generate significant income. Research the various monetization options—affiliate marketing, sponsored posts, digital products, and so on—within your potential niche to ensure there's a clear path to revenue.

Competition is another factor to weigh. Ideally, you want to find a niche that's underserved. But in reality, most lucrative niches will have some level of competition. Instead of shying away from competition, look for gaps in the content that exists. What can you offer that others aren't? Maybe it's your unique voice, specialized knowledge, or even a novel content format like podcasts or infographics.

Once you've narrowed down your options, put your ideas to the test. Create a few blog posts or social media updates around the topics you're considering. Gauge the reactions, shares, and engagement they receive. This initial testing phase can provide valuable insights into what resonates with your audience.

Embrace your uniqueness. Your personal experiences, insights, and authority in your chosen niche can set you apart from the sea of bloggers out there. Don't underestimate the value of your unique perspective. People are not only looking for information; they're looking for connection, relatability, and authenticity.

Think long-term. A niche that excites you today should still be engaging five years down the road. Trends come and go, but choosing a topic that you have a long-term interest in will sustain both your enthusiasm and, ultimately, your blog's staying power.

After you've done your homework and tested the waters, make an informed decision, but also trust your gut. Sometimes intuition leads us in the right direction even when the data seems inconclusive. Remember, no niche is set in stone. As you grow and gain more insights, you can always pivot slightly to better fit your audience's needs and interests.

To sum up, finding your niche requires a blend of self-awareness, market research, and a dash of intuition. It's the foundation of a successful blogging career and a key step towards building a sustainable source of passive income. So take your time, explore, experiment, and choose a niche that aligns your passions with profitability. Your future self—and your bank account—will thank you.

Content Creation and SEO

Creating compelling content is at the heart of any successful blog. This section will walk you through the nuances of content creation and how SEO (Search Engine Optimization) can skyrocket your blog's visibility, turning casual visitors into loyal readers, and ultimately, earning you a steady stream of income. The goal is not just to churn out pieces but to create value-driven content that resonates with your audience and ranks well on search engines.

Before diving into content creation, it's essential to understand your audience. Who are they? What problems are they facing? What solutions are they searching for online? Knowing these details helps tailor your content to meet their needs. Start by creating reader personas—fictional characters that represent different segments of your audience. These personas will guide you in writing posts that solve their specific problems and answer their questions.

When it comes to idea generation, the sky's the limit. Jot down every topic that comes to mind, then use tools like Google Trends, AnswerThePublic, and BuzzSumo to validate and expand on these ideas. These platforms provide insights into what people are searching for and talking about, giving you a clearer picture of trending topics in your niche. Your goal is to identify gaps in available content and fill them with unique, high-quality posts.

Now, let's get into the heart of content creation. Crafting a blog post goes beyond writing. It involves research, planning, drafting, and editing. Start with a strong headline that catches attention while being descriptive enough to tell readers what the post is about. Write an engaging introduction that hooks the reader; use anecdotes, statistics, or questions to draw them in. As you move into the body, break your content into digestible sections using subheadings, bullet points, and images. This not only improves readability but also makes your content more SEO-friendly.

Speaking of SEO, this is where the magic happens. SEO isn't just about stuffing your posts with keywords. It's about strategically using them to signal relevance to search engines. Start with keyword research. Tools like Ahrefs, SEMrush, and Google's Keyword Planner can help identify high-volume keywords relevant to your niche. Incorporate these keywords naturally within your title, headings, and throughout the body of your post. But remember, readability should always come first.

On-page SEO is equally important. This involves optimizing various elements within your posts. Use your primary keyword in the title tag, meta description, and URL. Google's algorithms also favor longer content, but quality trumps quantity. Aim for posts between 1,500 to 2,500 words that are rich in information and provide deep dives into the topic. Internal linking to other relevant posts on your blog can improve the user experience and keep readers engaged longer. Additionally, adding alt text to images helps search engines understand the content of the images, which can also improve your SEO ranking.

Your blog's loading speed also matters for SEO. A slow blog can frustrate users and lead to higher bounce rates, which negatively impact your search engine ranking. Compress images, use caching plugins, and consider a Content Delivery Network (CDN) to ensure that your blog loads quickly. Mobile optimization is another crucial factor. With a growing number of users accessing content through mobile devices, a responsive design can significantly improve user experience.

Content creation is not a one-off task but a continuous process. Regularly updating your blog with fresh content signals to search engines that your site is active and valuable. It also keeps your audience coming back for more. A content calendar can be a lifesaver here, helping you plan posts weeks in advance and ensuring you publish consistently.

Another aspect to consider is guest posting. Writing articles for other popular blogs in your niche can help you build backlinks, which are crucial for SEO. Backlinks act as endorsements from other sites, signaling to search engines that your content is credible and authoritative. Make sure the sites you're guest posting on are reputable; spammy backlinks can do more harm than good.

Don't underestimate the power of social media as part of your SEO strategy. Sharing your blog posts on platforms like Facebook, Twitter, and LinkedIn can drive traffic to your site and increase the odds of your content being shared by others. Utilize social sharing buttons on your blog to make it easy for readers to spread the word. Engaging with your audience on these platforms can also provide additional insights into what content resonates with them, offering new ideas for future posts.

Analytics play a crucial role in refining your content and SEO strategies. Tools like Google Analytics and Google Search Console offer insights into how your blog is performing. Track metrics such as page views, click-through rates, and bounce rates to understand what's working and what needs improvement. User behavior reports can show you how visitors interact with your blog, providing clues about which parts of your content are most engaging or where they might be losing interest.

Monetizing your blog often starts with building a strong foundation of high-quality content that is also optimized for search engines. Once you have a substantial amount of traffic, consider avenues like affiliate marketing, sponsored posts, and selling digital products to turn your blog into a revenue stream. But remember, none of this is possible without a focus on creating content that offers real value to your audience while being discoverable through SEO.

Content creation and SEO are deeply intertwined. One can't truly succeed without the other. By putting in the effort to produce valuable content that's also optimized for search engines, you're setting your blog up not just for higher traffic but for sustained success. Patience and persistence are key. SEO results may take time, but the payoff in terms of increased visibility and income potential can be substantial.

In summary, mastering content creation and SEO is essential for building a blog that earns. Engage with your audience, research diligently, prioritize readability, and stay updated with SEO best practices. The road isn't easy, but with commitment and the right strategies, the rewards can be immense.

Monetizing Your Blog

So, you've got a blog up and running, the content is rich, and the audience is beginning to grow. The next logical step is to turn those pages and posts into a revenue-generating machine. Monetizing your blog isn't just about slapping some ads on your homepage and calling it a day; it's an intricate blend of strategy, creativity, and understanding your audience. Done right, your blog can become a sustainable source of passive income.

First thing you need to know is that there are various methods to monetize a blog, and it's best to diversify your income streams. This means mixing and matching different strategies to see what works best for your specific niche and audience. Some methods may bring in smaller amounts of money consistently, while others might result in significant revenue spikes depending on the time of year, trending topics, or other factors. Let's dive into the most effective ways to monetize your blog.

Display Advertising

One of the most common ways to monetize a blog is through display advertising. Services like Google AdSense, Media.net, and other ad networks make it relatively straightforward to place ads on your blog. These platforms automatically match ads to your site's content and visitors.

The income from display ads usually depends on the number of visitors, niches, and the quality of the content. Commonly, revenue is calculated through models like Cost Per Click (CPC) or Cost Per Thousand Impressions (CPM). It's important to note that while display ads can generate consistent income, they can also slow down your site if not managed well, affecting user experience.

Affiliate Marketing

Affiliate marketing is a golden goose for many bloggers. The idea is simple: you promote other people's products on your blog, and you get a commission for every sale made through your referral link. To make it work, it's important to choose products that are relevant to your content and genuinely useful to your audience.

Sign up for affiliate programs through networks like Amazon Associates, ShareASale, or CJ Affiliate. Write comprehensive product reviews, tutorial posts, or listicles featuring these products. You can place affiliate links within these posts or even create a dedicated resources page. Tracking the success of these links through your affiliate dashboard is crucial for optimizing your strategies.

Selling Digital Products

Digital products are an excellent source of passive income because they often require a one-time effort to create but can be sold repeatedly. These include e-books, online courses, templates, and software. If you have expertise in a particular area, consider packaging that knowledge into a digital format.

Platforms like Teachable, Udemy, and Gumroad make it easy to sell digital products. You can promote these products through your blog posts, email newsletters, and social media channels. Remember, the value of the product must be evident in your promotion, offering solutions to your audience's problems or enhancing their skills.

Sponsored Posts and Reviews

Once your blog gains traction and a significant following, brands may approach you for sponsored posts or reviews. This involves writing about a product or service in return for compensation. It's a win-win: the brand gets exposure to your audience, and you earn money for your endorsement.

Transparency is essential in sponsored content. Always disclose if a post is sponsored to maintain trust with your readers. Additionally, only accept sponsorships from brands that align with your values and would genuinely benefit your audience. A well-written sponsored post can blend seamlessly with your regular content, enriching rather than detracting from the user experience.

Membership and Subscription Models

Creating a membership or subscription area for your blog can generate steady, recurring revenue. Offer exclusive content, early access to new posts, or even one-on-one coaching sessions as part of the membership perks. Platforms like Patreon or Memberful can help you set up and manage these subscriptions.

For this to work, you need a loyal audience willing to pay for premium content. Focus on building community and delivering unique value that cannot be found in your regular blog posts.

Offering Services

If you've cultivated expertise in your niche, consider offering services like consulting, writing, social media management, or web design. Display a dedicated page on your blog outlining the services you offer, and use your content to showcase your skills to potential clients.

Offering services can be a lucrative way to monetize your blog, but it's less passive compared to other methods. As you grow, consider creating systems to automate inquiries, bookings, and even some client interactions to free up your time.

Donations and Crowdfunding

If your audience finds immense value in your content, they may be willing to support you through donations or crowdfunding. Sites like Ko-fi and Buy Me a Coffee allow your readers to make small donations as a token of their appreciation. Alternatively, you can run larger crowdfunding campaigns for specific projects or expansions.

This method works best if you have a strong, engaged community that genuinely values your work. Transparency about how the funds will be used can encourage more people to contribute.

Email Marketing

Don't underestimate the power of a strong email list. Building an email list lets you communicate directly with your most loyal readers.

Through email marketing, you can promote your blog, affiliate products, digital goods, and more. A tool like Mailchimp or ConvertKit can help you manage your campaigns effectively.

Segment your audience based on their interests and tailor your messaging accordingly. Providing exclusive content or special offers to your email subscribers can drive high conversion rates and significantly boost your blog's revenue potential.

Effective monetization requires a mix of these strategies. It involves regular tracking of what works and what doesn't. Utilize tools like Google Analytics to gain insights into your audience's behavior and preferences, allowing you to tweak your approach strategically. The ultimate goal is to create a balance where your audience feels they're receiving value, and you're generating consistent revenue.

The journey to monetization is a marathon, not a sprint. By diversifying your income streams and staying adaptable, you can create a sustainable blogging business that earns—and keeps earning—passive income.

Chapter 7:
Passive Income through Licensing

Now that we've explored various foundational strategies for generating passive income, let's delve into licensing—a lucrative yet often overlooked avenue. Licensing allows you to leverage your intellectual property, like inventions, designs, or even creative works, by permitting others to use them in exchange for a fee or royalty. It's a win-win; companies get to utilize fresh ideas without the R&D costs, and you receive ongoing income without the day-to-day grind. Imagine you've created a novel design for a product or even written a catchy jingle. Instead of manufacturing it yourself, you could license it to a company that handles the production and sales, while you sit back and enjoy the steady flow of royalties. The key is to have something unique and marketable, then target companies that would benefit from your innovation. By understanding the process of how to license your ideas effectively, you're opening a door to a stream of income that can keep flowing long after the initial effort has been made.

What Is Licensing?

Licensing is a fascinating avenue for generating passive income, primarily because it allows you to capitalize on something you've already created without extra effort on your part. Imagine you've invented a unique product, designed a piece of intellectual property, or developed a compelling piece of software. Instead of manufacturing, distributing, and marketing it yourself, you can license it. This way, you're giving someone else the right to use, produce, or sell your creation while you sit back and collect a royalty.

So, what exactly does licensing entail? At its core, licensing is a legal agreement where you, as the license owner (or licensor), grant someone else (the licensee) the right to use your intellectual property or product under predefined conditions. These conditions can include how long the license lasts, where it can be used, and how much the licensee will pay you for the privilege.

To start, it's essential to understand why someone would want to license your creation in the first place. The main advantage for a licensee is that they avoid the time, effort, and cost needed to develop something new from scratch. For you, as the licensor, it's an opportunity to earn passive income from an existing asset. This win-win situation is why licensing can be so lucrative if done right.

There are various types of intellectual properties you can license. Patents, trademarks, copyrights, and trade secrets are the big ones. Each comes with its own set of rules, protection periods, and potential for generating income. For instance, a patent on a groundbreaking invention might bring in higher royalties but has more rigorous filing and maintenance requirements compared to a copyright, which could protect something like a song or a book.

When it comes to the mechanics of licensing agreements, they can get quite detailed. Agreements usually spell out the royalty rates, which are often a percentage of the sales. These percentages can range widely, depending on the industry and the perceived value of your creation. Terms also cover aspects like exclusivity. Will you grant exclusive rights to one licensee, or will multiple parties be allowed to license your property? Exclusive agreements might bring in higher royalties, but non-exclusive ones can broaden your income stream.

Let's dive into some real-world applications. Take software licensing as an example. When you develop a piece of software, you can license it out to companies or individual users. These licenses can be per-user, per-device, or site-wide, providing you with various income streams from a single product. The licensee benefits from a ready-made solution while you enjoy recurring revenue—it's like hitting the jackpot every time someone installs your software.

Then there's the world of artistic creations—think of musicians who license their songs for use in movies, TV shows, or advertisements. Licensing in this sphere is often multi-tiered, with different fees for different levels of usage. A song used in a blockbuster movie will command a higher royalty compared to one used in a local commercial. But the principle remains the same: once the licensing agreement is in place, the musician continues to earn passive income without lifting a finger.

Another fascinating realm of licensing is consumer products. Imagine you've designed a unique piece of technology. Instead of venturing into manufacturing, you license the design to a company that has the resources to produce and distribute it. While they handle the heavy lifting, you'd earn a royalty on each unit sold. It's a straightforward way to leverage your creativity and inventiveness into continuous revenue.

Don't think that licensing is only for high-flying inventors and artists. Even content creators can tap into this income stream. For instance, if you create an online course filled with valuable insights, you can license that course to educational institutions or online learning platforms. They get quality content to offer their students, and you receive a steady revenue stream without having to teach the course over and over again.

To get started with licensing, there are several steps you'll need to take. First, make sure your intellectual property is protected through patents, trademarks, or copyrights. This is crucial because an unprotected asset is vulnerable to being copied without compensation. Once you have your protections in place, you'll want to draft a solid licensing agreement. This is best done with the help of a lawyer who specializes in intellectual property law. The agreement should detail all the important terms: payment, duration, territory, and exclusivity.

Next, find potential licensees. This step can involve reaching out directly to companies in your industry, attending trade shows, or using licensing agents who can connect you with interested parties. Your pitch should highlight not only the merits of your intellectual property but also the commercial benefits of licensing it. Companies are more likely to be interested if they can see a clear path to profitability.

Negotiating the licensing deal is another critical step. This is where you'll discuss royalties, as well as other terms. It's a good idea to go into negotiations with a clear understanding of what your intellectual property is worth and keep a fair but firm stance on key points. Once an agreement is reached, make sure it is formalized in a legal contract to protect both parties involved.

Monitoring and managing the agreement doesn't end with the signing. Periodically, you'll need to check in and ensure that royalties are being paid timely and accurately. Some agreements include audit clauses, allowing the licensor to review the licensee's financial records to confirm that all dues are being met.

It's also important to stay vigilant about the relevance of your intellectual property. Market conditions change, and so do the demands for certain products. Licensing agreements often include clauses for renegotiation or renewal. Pay close attention to these terms and be prepared to adjust the agreement to reflect current market values.

The power of licensing lies in its ability to turn a one-time effort into a continuous income stream. It's like creating a money-making machine that keeps running long after you've flicked the switch. By grasping the nuances of what licensing is and how it works, you position yourself to capitalize on your creations continually, turning your ingenuity into a gift that keeps on giving.

How to License Your Ideas

If you have a unique idea, invention, or creative work, you may be sitting on a potential goldmine. Licensing your ideas can be a highly lucrative form of passive income. It's a method where you retain ownership of your intellectual property (IP) while allowing others to use, manufacture, or distribute your idea in exchange for royalties. This can range from product designs and software to music and written content. But where do you start? This section will guide you through the essential steps for successfully licensing your ideas.

First and foremost, you need to protect your idea. This usually means getting a patent, trademark, or copyright, depending on the nature of your idea. Patents are typically used for inventions, trademarks for brands and logos, and copyrights for artistic works. Securing legal protection gives you the upper hand in negotiations and ensures that your intellectual property isn't misused or copied without consequences.

Once your idea is protected, the next step is to identify potential licensees. These are companies or individuals who might be interested in using your idea. The key is to target those who are likely to see the most value from your concept. For instance, if you've developed a new kitchen gadget, your target licensees might be established kitchenware brands. Conduct market research to identify these potential partners, leveraging industry reports, trade shows, and online directories.

Now comes the pitching process. Your pitch should be concise and compelling, outlining the benefits and market potential of your idea. Typically, a pitch will include an executive summary, a detailed description of the idea, any preliminary sales data or market research, and visual aids such as prototypes or diagrams. Confidence is crucial here, as is preparedness to answer any questions that the potential licensee might have.

Sharing a prototype or proof of concept can further elevate your pitch. Many potential licensees want to see something tangible before they commit. A working model can make your idea more attractive and demonstrate its feasibility. If developing a prototype isn't feasible, detailed sketches, 3D renderings, or software demos can suffice.

Next comes the negotiation stage. It's essential to have a clear understanding of what you want from the deal. Typically, licensing agreements include an initial licensing fee, ongoing royalties (a percentage of each sale), or a combination of both. Royalties usually range from 2% to 10% of net sales, though this can vary widely depending on the industry and the uniqueness of your idea. Be prepared to negotiate terms such as the royalty rate, duration of the agreement, territory (geographical scope), and exclusivity (whether the licensee is the only one who can use your idea).

Here's where having a good legal advisor pays off. Licensing agreements can be complicated, and you'll want to ensure that the contract protects your interests. Your lawyer can help draft and review the agreement, making sure that all essential terms are covered. This includes intellectual property ownership, payment terms, quality control standards, and provisions for resolving disputes.

It's also important to have an exit strategy. Licensing agreements typically have clauses that allow for termination under specific conditions, such as non-performance by the licensee or breach of contract. Understanding these terms up front can save you from future headaches and ensure that you can reclaim your intellectual property if the arrangement doesn't work out.

Once the agreement is in place, you can start reaping the benefits of your work. The licensee will manufacture, market, and sell the product, while you earn royalties. However, don't just sit back completely. It's crucial to monitor the licensee's performance. Make sure they're adhering to the terms of the agreement, especially concerning quality and sales reporting. Regularly reviewing sales reports ensures that you're receiving the correct royalty payments.

You might also want to think about expanding your licensing efforts. Licensing doesn't have to be a one-and-done deal. If your idea is versatile, consider licensing it to multiple companies, perhaps in different industries or geographical regions. This can significantly boost your income and spread the risk if one licensee underperforms.

Furthermore, networking plays a critical role in successful licensing. Often, the best opportunities come through professional networks and industry contacts. Attending trade shows, joining professional organizations, and participating in online forums related to your industry can open doors to potential licensing deals. Building relationships with industry insiders helps you stay informed about who might be looking for new ideas and innovations.

Lastly, keep innovating. The marketplace is competitive, and what's hot today might be old news tomorrow. Continually refine your ideas and stay abreast of industry trends. A portfolio of IP assets is far more valuable than a single idea, both in terms of income potential and negotiating power.

Licensing your ideas might sound daunting, but with careful planning, solid legal advice, and persistent effort, it can become a significant stream of passive income. The key is to approach it methodically, protect your interests, and keep your eyes open for opportunities. Happy licensing!

Chapter 8:
Automating Your Business

Imagine a world where your business runs like a well-oiled machine, even while you're lounging on a beach or catching up on sleep. That's the magic of automation. By leveraging automated systems and tools, you can streamline your operations and free up both time and mental energy. Whether it's through email marketing campaigns that send themselves, or e-commerce platforms that handle inventory and shipping, automation ensures your business activities keep humming along without constant oversight. It's not just about efficiency; it's about reclaiming your time and multiplying your impact. Dive into automation, and you'll find it's an indispensable ally in growing your passive income streams and crafting a life that balances work and freedom effortlessly.

The Power of Automation

It's amazing what happens when businesses embrace automation. It's like pushing the fast-forward button on your productivity without compromising the quality of your work. Automation can turn even the most mundane tasks into streamlined processes, freeing up time and mental energy that's better spent on strategy and growth.

First off, let's talk about efficiency. When you automate repetitive tasks, you're essentially handing them off to a machine that won't get tired, make mistakes, or need a coffee break. Think about all those hours you currently spend on things like generating invoices, managing inventory, or even simple social media posts. Now imagine having those hours back to brainstorm your next big idea.

Time is money, as they say, and automation gives you more of both. By automating your business processes, you reduce the chance of human error, which can be costly both in terms of time and resources. Errors lead to rework, and rework slows you down. When the software handles these tasks, it executes them perfectly every time.

Beyond efficiency, automation can drastically improve your customer experience. When orders are processed faster, customers notice. When they get timely responses to their inquiries, they feel valued. Smart businesses use automation to create personalized customer experiences at scale. For example, chatbots can answer common questions instantly, providing the information customers need without making them wait. This responsiveness can make your customers feel like they're getting VIP treatment.

Of course, the journey to successful automation isn't without its bumps. Implementing these systems requires an initial investment of time and money. There's a learning curve, and it can be tempting to stick with your manual processes simply because they're familiar. But once you get through the setup and initial adjustment period, the long-term benefits will far outweigh these preliminary hurdles.

Picture a sales funnel, from lead generation to conversion. Automation can seamlessly guide potential clients through this funnel, ensuring no one slips through the cracks. Tools can track interactions, follow up with prospects, and even schedule appointments without any manual effort. It's like having a well-oiled machine that runs around the clock, even when your team is off the clock.

Let's not forget the power of data in automation. With automated tools, you can collect and analyze vast amounts of information quickly. This data helps you make more informed decisions, helping you pivot your strategy swiftly when needed. In the long run, this data-driven approach can give you a competitive edge in the marketplace.

Speaking of data, automated systems are also fantastic for tracking performance metrics. When you have a clear picture of how your business is performing in real-time, it's easier to identify areas for improvement. For instance, you can quickly see which products are selling well and which aren't, allowing you to make quick adjustments to your inventory.

Furthermore, consider the role of automation in marketing. Automated email campaigns, for example, can nurture leads by sending personalized messages at the right time, without you lifting a finger. These tools can segment your audience, ensuring that each recipient gets content that's relevant to them. Imagine the ripple effect this could have on your engagement rates and, eventually, your sales.

One key area where automation shines is in customer relationship management (CRM). Automated CRM systems can follow up with leads, schedule reminders, and even offer insights into customer behavior. This means you can focus more on building relationships and less on managing them. Moreover, CRM systems integrated with AI can predict customer needs and preferences, helping you offer a more personalized experience.

Let's pivot a bit and talk about the human aspect. While automation handles routine tasks, your team can focus on more complex, creative endeavors. This not only boosts morale but also fosters innovation. Employees engaged in meaningful work are more likely to bring fresh ideas to the table, which can propel your business forward.

In addition to boosting morale, automation can significantly reduce stress. Endless to-do lists and constant firefighting can drain even the most dedicated team members. By automating routine, repetitive tasks, you're reducing the number of balls your team has to juggle, allowing them to concentrate on what truly matters. This approach can also reduce burnout and turnover, which are costly in terms of both time and money.

One often-overlooked benefit of automation is scalability. As your business grows, the demands on your time and resources will increase. Manual processes that worked when you had a handful of customers can become unmanageable with a hundred. Automation lets you scale your operations efficiently, ensuring your processes remain robust and effective even as you expand.

Financial management is another area ripe for automation. Imagine a system that tracks expenses, sends invoices, manages payroll, and even handles taxes automatically. This wouldn't just save time; it would also reduce errors and ensure compliance with regulations. The more streamlined your financial operations, the easier it is to manage cash flow and plan for the future.

Automation can also make compliance easier. With regulations constantly changing, keeping up can be a headache. Automated systems can alert you to new requirements and even handle some compliance tasks for you. This reduces the risk of penalties and ensures that you're always in line with the latest rules.

So, how do you get started with automation? Begin by identifying the tasks that consume the most time and offer the least value when done manually. These are prime candidates for automation. Next, look for tools and software that can handle these tasks. Start small, perhaps with one or two processes, and gradually scale up as you get comfortable.

There's an abundance of automation tools available, catering to various aspects of business operations. From marketing and sales to customer service and finance, the options are nearly limitless. Research to find tools that integrate well with your existing systems and processes. This will help avoid the disruptions that can come from adopting new technologies.

Before you make any decisions, consider the return on investment (ROI). While some tools have a high upfront cost, their long-term benefits usually justify the expense. Calculate the time and money you'll save, and weigh this against the cost of the tool. Most often, you'll find that the investment pays off within months.

Finally, keep in mind that automation is not a set-it-and-forget-it solution. You'll need to periodically review and adjust your automated processes to ensure they are still meeting your needs. This brings us back to the power of data. Use the metrics you gathered to refine your strategies continually. Think of it as a cycle: automating to save time, using that saved time to innovate, and then using innovation to drive further automation.

In summary, the power of automation lies not just in the time and cost savings but also in the potential for growth, improved customer experiences, and enhanced employee satisfaction. By embracing automation, you can free yourself from the daily grind, allowing you to focus on what truly matters: building a sustainable, passive income-generating business. So take the plunge, adopt automation, and watch your business transform in ways you never imagined.

Tools and Resources for Automating Your Income

When it comes to automating your business, the right tools and resources can make all the difference. They streamline operations, save time, and can even help you scale faster. Whether you're handling real estate investments, managing a stock portfolio, or running an online business, automation tools can take the repetitive tasks off your hands, allowing you to focus on growth strategies and innovation.

Let's start with real estate investments. Property management software is a must-have for landlords and real estate investors. These tools can automate rent collection, maintenance requests, and tenant screening. Some popular options include AppFolio, Buildium, and TenantCloud. They offer features like online rental applications, lease tracking, and even financial reporting, giving you a comprehensive solution to manage your properties more efficiently.

If you're looking to automate your stock investments, robo-advisors are a great resource. These automated financial advisors use algorithms to manage your investment portfolio. They can help rebalance your portfolio based on market conditions and your risk preferences. Top robo-advisors like Betterment, Wealthfront, and M1 Finance offer services such as tax-loss harvesting and retirement planning, making investing less hands-on for you.

For those diving into online businesses, a robust e-commerce platform is essential. Shopify, WooCommerce, and BigCommerce are excellent choices for setting up an online store. They offer integrations with various payment gateways, inventory management systems, and marketing tools to help automate sales and operations. Additionally, using dropshipping apps like Oberlo can further automate your supply chain by syncing your store with suppliers who fulfill orders on your behalf.

Digital marketing automation tools are also vital for online entrepreneurs. Platforms like HubSpot, Mailchimp, and ActiveCampaign can automate your email marketing, social media posts, and even customer relationship management (CRM). These tools can segment your audience, personalize your messages, and provide detailed analytics to help you fine-tune your marketing strategies. The result? More efficient campaigns and stronger customer engagement.

Content creators and bloggers can benefit enormously from automation as well. Tools like Hootsuite, Buffer, and CoSchedule allow you to schedule blog posts, social media updates, and even email newsletters in advance. This way, you can maintain a consistent content schedule without the constant manual input. Combine these with SEO tools like Ahrefs, SEMrush, or Moz, and you'll get automated keyword tracking, site audits, and backlink analysis to ensure your content reaches the right audience.

For those interested in affiliate marketing, affiliate management tools like ClickBank, CJ Affiliate, and ShareASale can help you track sales, manage relationships with affiliate partners, and generate reports to monitor performance. These platforms usually come with built-in analytics, allowing you to see which affiliates are driving the most traffic and sales.

Licensees who wish to automate can benefit from intellectual property management software. Tools such as Anaqua, Lecorpio, and CPA Global can automate tasks related to IP portfolio management, including tracking licensing agreements, renewing patents, and managing royalties. Automating these processes can help you stay compliant and maximize your earnings from intellectual property.

Financial management software is another critical tool for automating income management. Tools like QuickBooks, Xero, and FreshBooks can automate invoicing, expense tracking, and even payroll. This makes it easier to keep track of your finances, generate financial reports, and ensure you're staying on top of your accounting responsibilities. Integrating these with your bank accounts and other financial platforms further simplifies the process.

Automation isn't just limited to business operations. Personal finance apps like Mint, Personal Capital, and YNAB can help automate your budgeting, savings goals, and expense tracking. These tools can link to your bank accounts, credit cards, and investment accounts to provide a comprehensive view of your financial situation, helping you make informed decisions and avoid overspending.

Let's not forget about the power of AI and machine learning in automating your income. AI-driven analytics tools can help you predict market trends, identify investment opportunities, and even automate trading. Platforms like Kensho, AlphaSense, and Sentieo use advanced algorithms to analyze vast amounts of data, offering insights that can give you a competitive edge.

Despite the many benefits, it's essential to choose tools that align with your needs and goals. Not every tool will be suitable for every type of business or investment. For instance, while a landlord might find property management software invaluable, it may not be useful for someone focused on dividend stocks. Always evaluate the features, pricing, and scalability of these tools before making a decision.

Additionally, it's worth noting that automation tools often come with a learning curve. Take the time to learn how to use these platforms effectively to maximize their potential. Many tools offer tutorials, customer support, and community forums to help you get started. Don't hesitate to invest time upfront to fully understand the functionalities and best practices.

Another critical aspect of automation is integrating these tools with one another. Using APIs and other integration services, you can create a seamless workflow that connects different parts of your business. For example, integrating your e-commerce platform with your email marketing tool can automate follow-up emails after a purchase, or syncing your accounting software with your bank accounts can provide real-time financial updates.

The use of virtual assistants (VAs) and outsourcing is another way to automate and delegate tasks. Platforms like Upwork, Fiverr, and Freelancer allow you to hire skilled professionals for various tasks ranging from customer service to content creation. While not strictly a 'tool,' virtual assistants can handle routine tasks, allowing you to focus on strategic planning and growth.

Lastly, don't overlook the importance of cybersecurity when automating your business. As you adopt more tools and platforms, ensuring your data is secure becomes crucial. Employing security measures such as two-factor authentication, regular software updates, and using reputable tools can help protect your business and personal information from cyber threats.

In summary, automating your business involves leveraging a variety of tools and resources designed to streamline operations, manage investments, and enhance productivity. From property management software and robo-advisors to digital marketing tools and financial management apps, there are numerous options available to help automate your income streams. Choosing the right tools, learning how to use them effectively, and integrating them for a seamless workflow can significantly boost your efficiency and help you achieve your passive income goals faster.

Chapter 9:
Managing Your Passive Income

As you dive deeper into your passive income journey, managing your earnings becomes a crucial task that can't be overlooked. Keeping track of your investments is more than just tallying numbers; it's about understanding where your money is generating the highest returns and where you might need to reallocate resources. A solid grasp on the performance metrics of each income stream helps in making informed decisions, ensuring you're maximizing your earnings. Equally important is dealing with taxes appropriately—knowing the tax implications of each type of passive income can save you a significant amount of headaches (and dollars) down the line. Remember, while setting up passive income streams might feel like crossing the finish line, managing them effectively is what truly influences your financial freedom journey.

Keeping Track of Your Investments

Investing is a journey, and like any journey, it requires regular check-ins and adjustments to ensure you're on the right path. You wouldn't set out on a road trip without a map or GPS, right? Similarly, keeping track of your investments is crucial to managing your passive income streams effectively. It's not just about putting your money into real estate, dividend stocks, or online businesses and then forgetting about it. You've got to monitor and pivot when necessary.

First off, let's talk about organization. You need to keep your investment records organized. It's easy to think you'll remember everything, but the reality is that investment portfolios can become a mess quickly. Use digital tools like spreadsheets or specialized accounting software to keep track of your investments. These tools allow you to see where your money is, how it's performing, and what changes might be necessary.

One of the most important facets of tracking your investments is performance monitoring. It's not enough to know where your money is invested; you need to know how well it's doing. Regularly review your statements and reports. For stock portfolios, many brokerages offer dashboards where you can see gains, losses, and overall performance at a glance. Real estate investments might require a bit more work, looking at rental yields, property values, and maintenance costs.

Next up is diversification – how spread out are your investments? Even if you've followed all the steps to build a diverse portfolio, things can change. Market conditions fluctuate, and what was once a solid investment might not hold the same promise today. By regularly reviewing your investment portfolio, you can ensure it's balanced and aligned with your risk tolerance and financial goals.

Notification and alert systems can be your best friends. Many investment platforms provide customizable alerts that notify you when an asset hits a certain price point or when there's significant news about a sector you're invested in. This real-time information can help you make informed decisions quicker, so you're not left behind as the markets move.

And let's not forget about rebalancing. Over time, your portfolio might shift out of alignment with your initial investment strategy due to market performance. Rebalancing involves selling off over-performing assets and buying under-performing ones to get back to your desired asset allocation. This ensures that you're not taking on more risk than you intended and helps to lock in gains.

Technology may assist, but ·human touch is essential. Regular consultations with financial advisors can provide perspectives that data alone cannot offer. They can help you understand complex market trends and advise on strategic changes to maximize returns or minimize risks. Their expertise is invaluable, especially in volatile markets.

Additionally, keep an eye on transaction costs. Over time, these can eat into your profits, especially if you're frequently buying and selling assets. Look for low-cost brokerage options and be mindful of fees related to your investments. It's about maximizing every dollar you're putting to work.

Tax implications are another essential consideration. Different investments come with different tax responsibilities. For example, dividend income is usually taxed at a lower rate than regular income, but it still needs to be reported. Real estate investments might offer tax advantages like depreciation, but you'll need detailed records to maximize these benefits. Always keep track of your gains and losses, and consult with a tax professional to make sure you're not leaving money on the table.

One more critical point is having access to liquidity. While some investments might lock your money for a certain period, having a portion of your portfolio that's easily accessible is wise. This ensures you can handle unexpected expenses without needing to sell off investments at suboptimal times.

Moreover, set regular review schedules. Whether it's quarterly or annually, these reviews ensure that you're not only tracking performance but also reassessing your goals. Sometimes, your financial goals may shift due to life changes, and your investment strategy might need to pivot accordingly.

Emotional detachment can't be overstated. Investments can fluctuate in value, and it's easy to get caught up in the emotional highs and lows. Keep a level head, stick to your plan, and resist the urge to make impulsive decisions. You're in this for the long haul, and a steady hand often fares better over time than one driven by short-term emotions.

Investing in educational resources also keeps you ahead of the curve. The financial landscape is always evolving, so regular reading or taking courses can provide new strategies and insights for maintaining a healthy portfolio. There's always more to learn, and staying informed can make a significant difference in how well you manage your investments.

Lastly, remember to celebrate your milestones. Financial growth can be slow and steady, but recognizing your achievements along the way can boost motivation and confidence. It's not just about reaching your ultimate goal of financial freedom; it's also about appreciating the journey and the progress you've made.

In summary, keeping track of your investments involves a mixture of technology, regular review, expert advice, understanding tax implications, and maintaining liquidity. The effort you put into tracking and managing your investments pays dividends, not just in financial returns but also in peace of mind, knowing that you're actively steering your financial future in the right direction.

Dealing With Taxes

When you're diving into the world of passive income, one of the biggest hurdles you'll encounter is managing your tax obligations. Navigating through tax requirements can be tricky, especially if you're juggling multiple streams of income. But don't worry, understanding the tax implications is essential for effectively managing your passive income. Neglecting this important aspect can lead to unexpected bills from the IRS, which let's be honest, nobody wants.

First things first, it's crucial to distinguish between passive income and active income for tax purposes. The IRS has specific definitions and rules about what counts as passive income. Generally, passive income includes earnings derived from rental properties, dividends, interest, and other investments. Active income, on the other hand, is money earned from performing a service, like wages or tips. Knowing these differences will help you manage your tax responsibilities more efficiently.

Now, let's talk about the types of passive income that will likely form part of your portfolio: rental income, dividends, and interest. Each of these has its specific tax implications. For example, rental income must be reported as part of your gross income on your tax return. You'll end up paying tax on this income, but the good news is you may be able to deduct related expenses like property repairs, mortgage interest, and property management fees.

When it comes to dividends, things can get a bit more complex. Dividends are generally classified as either ordinary or qualified. Ordinary dividends are taxed as regular income, which could be a significant percentage depending on your tax bracket. Qualified dividends, however, are taxed at the lower long-term capital gains tax rates. Knowing how your dividends are classified can save you money in the long run.

Interest income, like the kind you earn from savings accounts, bonds, or other investments, is typically taxable at your ordinary income rate. There's not much you can do to cushion the blow here, but proper documentation and reporting are essential to avoid any issues with the IRS.

Another crucial element to keep in mind is depreciation, particularly if you own rental properties. Depreciation allows you to deduct the cost of buying and improving a rental property. Divided over a period (usually 27.5 years for residential properties), this deduction can significantly reduce your taxable rental income. However, it's essential to understand the concept of recapture. When you sell the property, any depreciation you've claimed might be taxed at a higher rate. So, while depreciation offers immediate tax benefits, it could have long-term implications that you need to consider.

Let's not forget about deductions. Keeping track of your deductions can vastly reduce your taxable income. Expenses like property management fees, repairs, insurance, and even the cost of advertising your rental property can be deducted. For those involved in stock investments, any advisor fees and certain other investment-related expenses can also be deducted. Staying on top of these deductions requires meticulous record-keeping, but the payoff can be well worth the effort.

One useful tip is to keep separate bank accounts and credit cards for your passive income activities. This separation simplifies tracking and reporting, making tax season less of a headache. It also allows you to keep a clear record which is invaluable should you ever face an audit.

Tax planning should be a year-round endeavor, not just a last-minute scramble before April 15th. Regularly updating and revisiting your tax strategy ensures you're maximizing your benefits and minimizing your tax liabilities. Many high earners find it useful to meet with their accountants at least twice a year to discuss changes in income, upcoming expenses, and other factors that might impact their taxes.

Speaking of accountants, hiring a professional can be one of the best investments you make. While tax software is increasingly sophisticated, there's no replacement for expert advice tailored to your specific situation. A qualified tax professional can identify opportunities for tax savings that you might miss on your own. They can also help you navigate the complexities of tax law, including the numerous deductions and credits you might be eligible for.

An accountant can also assist you with more advanced strategies, like tax-loss harvesting. Essentially, this involves selling investments that have lost value to offset gains in other areas, thereby reducing your overall tax burden. However, this tactic requires careful planning and a solid understanding of both the tax code and your investment portfolio.

Understanding the tax implications of your passive income also means being aware of state taxes. Different states have different rules regarding how income is taxed. For instance, some states don't tax dividend income or capital gains, which can be a significant advantage for investors. Conversely, other states have high tax rates that can eat into your returns. Knowing the tax laws in your state and how they apply to your various income streams is crucial for effective tax planning.

If you've diversified your passive income streams internationally, you must also consider the implications of foreign taxes. Many countries where you invest will have their tax systems, and some income may be subject to foreign withholding taxes. Fortunately, the U.S. has treaties with many countries to help mitigate double taxation, and you can often get a foreign tax credit to offset some of what you've paid. However, this is another area where professional advice can be invaluable.

Finally, one aspect of taxes that often gets overlooked is the self-employment tax. If you generate passive income through activities like online businesses or rental properties where you provide substantial services, you might be subject to self-employment tax. This additional tax can significantly impact your overall tax liability, so it's essential to account for it when planning your finances.

In conclusion, dealing with taxes on your passive income can feel like walking through a maze. However, understanding the basics, keeping thorough records, planning year-round, and seeking professional advice can help you manage your taxes effectively. As your income streams grow and diversify, being proactive about your tax situation becomes even more critical. Don't let the complexity deter you; instead, view it as an essential component of your passive income journey. With the right approach, you can minimize your tax liabilities and keep more of what you earn, paving the way for financial freedom.

Chapter 10:
Scaling Up

So you've got your passive income streams humming along, but how do you take it to the next level? That's where scaling up comes into play. Scaling up involves knowing when to reinvest your earnings and diversify your passive income sources for greater financial stability and growth. It's about taking calculated risks and integrating more sophisticated strategies, like expanding into new markets or leveraging advanced tools and technologies. Maybe you're considering adding rental properties to your portfolio or upping your game with high-dividend stocks. The goal is not just to make more money but to create a more resilient financial ecosystem. By the end of this chapter, you'll have a roadmap for recognizing prime opportunities for reinvestment and methods to spread out your income sources, ensuring a balanced and prosperous financial future.

When to Invest More

Scaling up your passive income can be a thrilling, albeit challenging, experience. One of the most critical aspects of this journey is determining when to invest more. This decision can feel like standing on the edge of a cliff, uncertain if your next step will lead to a triumphant leap or a perilous plunge. But worry not, it's all about recognizing the signs and understanding your financial landscape.

Firstly, consider your current financial stability. Before you think about pouring more money into your investments, ensure that your emergency fund is robust. Financial experts typically recommend having three to six months' worth of living expenses saved up. This cushion gives you a safety net, protecting you from unforeseen circumstances like job loss or medical emergencies. If your emergency fund is in good shape, it can be a green light to start thinking about scaling up.

Another key indicator is the performance of your current investments. If your investments are consistently returning profits and growing, it might be time to consider allocating more funds. This doesn't just apply to stocks or real estate; it could be any passive income stream like an e-commerce business, digital products, or even a blog. Track your metrics diligently, whether that's ROI, traffic numbers, or monthly earnings. Positive trends often signal it's time to double down.

Evaluating market conditions is also crucial. Markets can be volatile, and timing is everything. Conduct thorough research to understand current trends, economic indicators, and potential future shifts. A favorable market can amplify your returns, whereas a downturn could magnify your losses. If experts predict growth in your chosen sector, it could be a prime opportunity to increase your investment.

Diversification is another aspect to consider when deciding to invest more. Instead of putting all your eggs in one basket, think about spreading your investments across different types of assets or income streams. This strategy reduces risk and increases the chance for higher returns. For instance, coupling real estate investments with dividend stocks or an online business can create a more balanced and resilient portfolio.

It's also worth mentioning the psychology of investing more. Many times, the hesitation to scale up stems from fear or previous setbacks. Psychological barriers can make us overly cautious, causing us to miss out on potential opportunities. It's important to strike a balance between prudent caution and bold investment. Reflect on your past experiences, learn from your mistakes, but don't let them paralyze you into inaction. Use them as stepping stones to make informed, confident decisions.

Assessing your financial goals can provide clarity. Are you aiming for long-term wealth accumulation, early retirement, or perhaps funding your children's education? Your goals can inform how aggressively you should invest. For long-term goals, a more aggressive approach may be warranted, considering you have the time to ride out market fluctuations. Conversely, for short-term targets, a conservative stance might be more suitable.

Cash flow also plays a significant role. If you have a healthy cash flow from your current passive income streams, it might be wise to reinvest a portion back into the business. Reinvesting profits can accelerate growth and compound your earnings. For instance, if your e-commerce business is thriving, using a part of the profits to enhance marketing efforts or expand inventory could exponentially increase future revenues.

Next, let's talk about expertise and knowledge. If you've become more knowledgeable about a particular type of investment, you're in a better position to scale up. For example, if you've spent years understanding the real estate market and have successfully managed several properties, investing more in this area makes sense. Your expertise reduces risk and increases the likelihood of higher returns.

Consulting with financial advisors can also provide valuable insights. Professionals can offer an objective perspective on when to invest more, based on your financial health and market conditions. They can help you develop a strategic plan, balancing risk and reward in alignment with your goals. Their advice can be particularly useful in complex scenarios, such as investing in international markets or advanced financial instruments.

Don't forget to consider the scalability of your passive income stream. Some streams are more scalable than others. For instance, digital products can be scaled infinitely with minimal additional cost, whereas physical real estate has limitations based on capital and market availability. Understanding the scalability potential can guide you on how much more to invest and what returns to expect.

Finally, monitor regulatory and tax implications. Any investment decision should consider the legal environment and tax consequences. New regulations can impact your returns, and tax liabilities can eat into your profits. Stay informed about changes in laws and how they might affect your investments.

In conclusion, knowing when to invest more is a combination of financial stability, market conditions, diversification, psychological readiness, and strategic planning. This decision requires a blend of caution and ambition, always backed by thorough research and informed judgment. Remember, there's no one-size-fits-all answer, but with careful consideration and planning, you can scale up your passive income streams effectively and achieve your financial goals. The journey is as crucial as the destination, and with each step, you're moving closer to financial freedom.

Diversifying Your Passive Income Streams

Diversifying your passive income streams is a crucial step when it comes to scaling up your financial game. It's like spreading out the roots of a tree; the broader they extend, the more nutrients they can absorb, and the stronger the tree grows. Likewise, when you diversify, you safeguard yourself against ups and downs in any single income source, ensuring that your financial ecosystem remains healthy and robust.

If you've put all your eggs in one basket, diversification might sound a bit nerve-wracking at first. But think of it as an adventure—a chance to explore new opportunities and avenues you've never considered before. While real estate, dividend stocks, and online businesses form the bedrock of many passive income portfolios, there's also room to experiment and discover less traditional paths that might align better with your skills and interests.

Let's start with the heavyweights—areas you're likely more familiar with: real estate and the stock market. If you're already earning from residential properties, consider adding a commercial property to your portfolio. Commercial properties, such as office buildings or retail spaces, often come with longer lease terms and higher rental yield. However, they may also require more complex management. The key is balance; by mixing residential with commercial real estate, you create a buffer against volatility in either market. It's the financial equivalent of hedging your bets.

Stocks are no different. If your portfolio is already producing dividends from traditional blue-chip companies, why not explore more niche sectors such as REITs, or Real Estate Investment Trusts? REITs offer a way to invest in real estate without the hassle of direct property management. Plus, they tend to pay high dividends, making them an attractive option for the income-focused investor. You may even consider high-growth sectors like technology or pharmaceuticals, which offer the potential for both capital gains and dividend income. However, always remember to balance risk with your long-term goals and risk tolerance.

Beyond these stalwarts, there are lesser-known avenues that can provide substantial passive income if navigated smartly. For instance, consider the intellectual property route by licensing your ideas. Whether it's a unique business concept, an innovative product, or creative work like music or ebooks, licensing can turn your intellectual effort into a continuous income stream. Licensing deals can vary from one-time payments to royalties based on sales, creating different levels of income security and growth potential.

Another thriving area worth diving into is digital entrepreneurship. It's a broad field, encompassing e-commerce, digital products, and affiliate marketing. If you already run an online store, think about selling digital products like e-books, online courses, or printables. These products often require an upfront time investment but can sell indefinitely, creating a solid stream of passive income without the hassle of inventory management. Similarly, affiliate marketing allows you to earn commissions by promoting other people's products, making it a win-win if you have a platform or a sizeable following.

One underrated gem in the world of passive income is peer-to-peer lending. Through specialized platforms, you can lend money directly to individuals or businesses, earning interest on your loans. While this comes with its set of risks, it also offers higher returns compared to traditional savings accounts and even some bonds. By selectively lending to creditworthy borrowers, you can create another diverse channel of passive income.

If you have a creative streak, art and collectibles can be another exciting frontier. Consider investing in art, rare coins, vintage cars, or even popular trading cards. While these require a keen eye and some initial knowledge to avoid pitfalls, the value of these assets can appreciate significantly over time. Not to mention, it's a uniquely thrilling way to diversify your portfolio.

The next step in diversification is the use of technology to automate your income streams. Tools and platforms have greatly democratized the ability to set up multiple passive income channels without being bogged down by management tasks. For instance, if you're running a blog or an e-commerce store, automation tools can handle everything from email marketing to inventory tracking. This allows you to scale up without proportionally scaling up your workload, freeing up time to cultivate new income streams.

Cryptocurrency is another modern avenue worth exploring. While it comes with high volatility, cryptocurrencies and blockchain technology present long-term investment potentials. For instance, staking your crypto to earn rewards or investing in blockchain projects that pay dividends can provide exposure to this emerging asset class. Just be sure to do extensive research, as the landscape is ever-changing and can be risky.

With all these options laid out, how do you decide where to focus your energy? The sweet spot lies in aligning these opportunities with your long-term goals and risk tolerance. Start by assessing your current passive income streams and identifying gaps or areas that could benefit from additional support. It's a bit like maintaining a well-balanced diet; variety doesn't just keep things interesting, it ensures you're not missing out on essential nutrients.

Take stock of your skills, interests, and resources. If you've got a knack for technology, diving into digital products or tech stocks may feel more natural. Alternatively, if you have a strong local network and a penchant for tangible assets, real estate or collectibles might be more appealing. Ultimately, the goal is to build a diversified portfolio that not only mitigates risk but also complements your lifestyle and aspirations.

Regularly review and adjust your portfolio. The financial landscape is dynamic, and what works for you today might not be as effective tomorrow. By staying informed and agile, you can navigate market shifts and capitalize on new opportunities as they arise. Consider annual or semi-annual reviews to reassess your strategies and make data-driven decisions. This proactive approach will keep your passive income streams flowing smoothly, ensuring long-term growth and stability.

So, roll up your sleeves and get ready to explore, adapt, and thrive. Diversifying your passive income streams isn't about juggling multiple sources haphazardly; it's a strategic approach to building a resilient and prosperous financial future. As you embark on this journey, remember that every step you take brings you closer to financial freedom.

Chapter 11:
The Pitfalls of Passive Income

As tempting as passive income sounds—the dream of earning money while you sleep—it's crucial to be aware of the potential pitfalls that come with it. One common mistake is underestimating the effort and time required to set up the initial streams, thinking it's all about quick and easy gains. People often fall into the trap of not diversifying their income sources, relying too heavily on a single source which could dry up or become unprofitable. Additionally, ignoring market trends or neglecting to regularly monitor and adjust your investments can leave you vulnerable to financial losses. It's also easy to get caught up in scams that promise high returns with little effort, only to find yourself losing your hard-earned money. Understanding these pitfalls can equip you with the foresight needed to navigate the complexities of building a sustainable passive income and ensure you're not blindsided by these common pitfalls.

Common Mistakes to Avoid

Diving into the world of passive income can be both exhilarating and daunting. While the allure of earning money with minimal ongoing effort is undeniably appealing, it's easy to trip up if you're not mindful. Here are some common mistakes that people often make on their journey to building passive income, and how you can avoid them.

One of the most frequent errors is not doing enough research before jumping in. Whether it's real estate, dividend stocks, or online businesses, each avenue has its complexities and nuances. Some assume that since the concept is "passive," the upfront effort might be minimal. Nothing could be further from the truth. It's crucial to understand the specifics of your chosen investment. For example, if you're investing in real estate, know the markets, property management requirements, and associated costs. In the case of stocks, you should understand the company's financial health and the market trends. Skipping this foundational research can lead you down a costly path.

Another common pitfall is underestimating the initial capital or effort required. Building a blog that generates significant ad revenue, for example, demands not just excellent content but consistent effort in SEO and social media marketing. Similarly, investing in high-dividend stocks requires substantial investment upfront to see meaningful returns. Without a clear understanding of these demands, people often give up too early, disillusioned by the lack of immediate results.

Many newbies also fall prey to the "set and forget" mindset. While passive income does aim to minimize ongoing work, it doesn't mean you can ignore your investments entirely. Markets fluctuate, trends change, and technology evolves. Neglecting to monitor and adjust your strategies can lead to diminishing returns. For instance, an e-commerce business requires periodic updates to stay competitive, while dividend stocks might need to be reevaluated based on the company's performance. Regular reviews can safeguard your income streams and help them grow.

Over-leveraging is another trap. It's tempting to maximize potential returns by borrowing money to invest, especially in real estate. However, this can be a double-edged sword. The market's volatility means that a downturn could leave you with not just diminished returns, but actual losses. Calculating risk and managing debt prudently is vital. A balanced portfolio that doesn't overly rely on borrowed funds is a safer bet.

People often neglect to diversify their investments. Relying on a single source of passive income is risky. The key to long-term financial stability lies in diversification. By spreading your investments across various avenues—such as real estate, stocks, and digital products—you mitigate the risk associated with any single investment's failure. This balance ensures that if one stream encounters turbulence, others can keep you afloat.

Failing to consider taxes can also eat into your income more than you might expect. Different types of passive income are taxed differently, and not accounting for this can lead to unpleasant surprises when tax season rolls around. Seek advice from a tax professional who can guide you on how to manage tax implications effectively. This preparation can help you maximize your net earnings.

An often-overlooked mistake is failing to set realistic goals. Many dive into the passive income world with dreams of overnight riches, only to be disappointed. It's crucial to set achievable milestones and understand that building significant passive income generally takes time. If you expect immediate results, you risk making rash decisions that can jeopardize your financial health.

Another pitfall is not continuously educating yourself. The landscape for passive income streams is ever-changing, and staying updated on the latest trends, tools, and strategies is essential. Be it through books, courses, or industry seminars, ongoing education ensures you stay ahead of the curve and can tweak your strategies for better returns.

Underestimating the importance of a support network is another common mistake. Networking with like-minded individuals can provide invaluable insights and opportunities. Surrounding yourself with others who have successfully navigated the passive income path can offer guidance, support, and even collaboration opportunities. This community can be a vital resource that helps you avoid pitfalls and leverage opportunities you might not have noticed on your own.

Lastly, don't ignore the emotional aspect. The patience required for passive income ventures can be frustrating. It's easy to lose motivation when the returns aren't immediate. Cultivating a long-term mindset and celebrating small wins can keep you engaged and focused on your end goal. Emotional resilience can be your best ally in this journey.

In summation, avoiding these common mistakes can significantly increase your chances of building a sustainable passive income. Be diligent in your research, patient in your approach, and proactive in managing your investments. Stay diversified, updated, and emotionally resilient. With these strategies in place, you'll be well on your way to achieving financial freedom.

How to Overcome Setbacks

In the journey towards building passive income, setbacks are inevitable. Every seasoned investor or online entrepreneur has faced obstacles that test their determination and prowess. What differentiates successful people from those who give up is their ability to overcome these setbacks and turn them into learning experiences. So, how can you effectively navigate the inevitable challenges on your passive income journey? Let's explore some practical strategies and mindset shifts that can help you stay on track.

Firstly, understand that setbacks are part of the process. It's easy to get discouraged when things don't go as planned, but remember that every mistake brings with it an opportunity to learn. If an investment doesn't yield the expected return, take the time to analyze what went wrong. Was it a lack of research? Did market conditions change unexpectedly? These answers can provide valuable insights for your future investments.

Emotional resilience is another critical component. When setbacks occur, it's natural to feel disappointment, frustration, or even fear. However, dwelling on these emotions can cloud your judgment and lead you to make rash decisions. Establishing a strong support network can be incredibly beneficial. Whether it's a mentor, a financial advisor, or a community of like-minded individuals, having someone to turn to for advice and encouragement can make all the difference.

Let's talk strategy. Diversification is your best friend when it comes to mitigating setbacks. Relying on a single source of passive income can be risky. If that source dries up, it can derail your entire financial plan. By spreading your investments across different types of passive income—such as real estate, stocks, and online businesses—you reduce the risk of losing everything simultaneously. This way, even if one avenue underperforms, others can help keep you afloat.

Don't underestimate the power of continuous learning. The world of passive income is ever-evolving, with new opportunities and challenges arising constantly. Staying updated on market trends, technological advancements, and industry best practices can give you a competitive edge. Consider dedicating time each month to read books, attend webinars, or participate in online courses. Knowledge is your most potent tool for overcoming setbacks.

Another important aspect is financial planning. Having an emergency fund can be a lifesaver when facing unexpected downturns. Ideally, this fund should cover three to six months of your living expenses. It's your safety net in case your rental property sits vacant longer than expected, or your dividend stocks take a hit. By having this buffer, you can afford to wait out rough patches without plunging into debt or making hasty decisions.

Automation can also play a crucial role in overcoming setbacks. It can free up your time and reduce the chances of human error. Tools that automate tasks like tracking investments, managing rental properties, or handling online business operations can ensure you're making the most efficient use of your time. Plus, automation tools often come with analytics features, providing you with real-time data that helps in quick decision-making during challenging times.

Perseverance is key. Setbacks might tempt you to abandon your passive income projects altogether, especially when you're not seeing the desired returns immediately. However, persistence often pays off. Keep in mind the long-term benefits that drove you to start this journey in the first place. Reflecting on your initial motivations can rekindle your passion and help you push through tough times.

Goal adjustment may also be necessary. Sometimes, setbacks can reveal that your initial goals were overly ambitious or not aligned with current realities. That's perfectly fine. Being flexible with your objectives can help you adapt to new conditions and still make progress, even if it's at a different pace or on a modified path. Recalibrating your goals based on newly acquired insights can turn a setback into a stepping stone.

Effective time management can help you juggle multiple responsibilities without feeling overwhelmed. Segregate your tasks based on priority and deadlines. Use planners or apps to keep track of your daily, weekly, and monthly goals. By managing your time efficiently, you're more likely to tackle setbacks proactively instead of reactively.

Lastly, acknowledge and celebrate small victories. Setbacks often overshadow the progress you've made, making it difficult to see how far you've come. Take the time to note your achievements, no matter how minor they seem. These wins can boost your morale and give you the motivation needed to face bigger challenges.

In conclusion, setbacks are not the end of your passive income journey; they're merely detours that offer valuable lessons and opportunities for growth. By maintaining emotional resilience, seeking support, diversifying income streams, continuously learning, planning financially, leveraging automation, remaining persistent, adjusting goals, managing time effectively, and celebrating small victories, you can turn setbacks into stepping stones toward achieving lasting financial freedom.

Chapter 12:
Success Stories

In our journey to unlocking the secrets of passive income, there's nothing quite as inspiring as hearing about real-world successes. From a young couple who turned a modest real estate venture into a thriving multi-property portfolio, to a single mother who diversified her investments between dividend stocks and an online business, these stories highlight the transformative potential of passive income. One tale recounts the meteoric rise of a digital nomad who leveraged affiliate marketing to travel the world while earning a steady income. Each narrative demystifies the path to passive income, illustrating that with the right strategies and a bit of perseverance, achieving financial freedom is not just a dream but an attainable reality. These heartfelt anecdotes serve not only as motivation but also as a practical guide, showing firsthand how diverse approaches can lead to extraordinary outcomes.

Real-Life Examples of Passive Income Success

Diving straight into the heart of the matter, let's explore some real-life stories that will not only inspire but also offer tangible proof that passive income can transform lives. The beauty of these examples lies in their diversity, demonstrating how different strategies can work for different people. Whether you're considering real estate, stocks, or online businesses, there's a success story that can provide insights and motivation.

First up, meet Sarah, a single mom from Texas who turned her life around by investing in rental properties. When Sarah's divorce left her financially uncertain, she knew she needed to create a stable future for her kids. Instead of wallowing in despair, she educated herself about real estate through online courses and local seminars. With an initial investment saved from her modest salary, Sarah bought her first rental property. Fast forward five years, she now owns five rental homes, generating over $5,000 a month in passive income. Her journey wasn't easy—she dealt with tenant issues and property repairs, but her perseverance paid off big time.

Then there's Mike, a corporate worker from New York, who decided he wanted more from life than just the daily grind. He dove into the world of dividend stocks after learning about it from a colleague. Initially, Mike started small, investing just a couple of hundred dollars each month. He meticulously researched companies with a history of paying consistent dividends and reinvested those earnings back into his portfolio. Over 15 years, Mike built a diversified portfolio that now gives him $30,000 annually in dividends—enough to cover most of his living expenses. He didn't quit his job right away, but the financial cushion allowed him to take a sabbatical and travel, enriching his life in ways that a corporate pay raise never could.

Let's not forget about Linda, who turned her blogging passion into a goldmine. Linda always loved writing and sharing her ideas but never thought she'd make money from it. She started a blog about eco-friendly living, focusing on actionable tips for her readers. By using SEO techniques and maintaining a consistent posting schedule, her blog's traffic grew exponentially. Through affiliate marketing and sponsored posts, Linda now earns a significant passive income. Her blog generates around $10,000 a month, and all she had to do was create content she loved. The key takeaway here was consistency and understanding her niche audience.

In the realm of digital products, we have Alex, a software developer who created a "to-do list" app over a weekend hackathon. Initially, he released it for free, but after seeing its popularity, he introduced a premium version with added features. Alex didn't spend a dime on marketing; instead, he relied on word-of-mouth and positive reviews. Within a year, his app was bringing in $50,000 annually. What made Alex's story unique is that he continued working his regular job while his app earned passive income, offering him the financial flexibility to explore other projects.

Another fascinating story is that of Brenda and Steve, a couple from Florida, who leveraged the power of e-commerce. They started by selling handmade candles on Etsy and later expanded to their website. To scale their business without compromising on quality, they automated many processes like inventory management and email marketing. Today, their small venture has blossomed into a full-fledged online store, bringing in an impressive six-figure passive income. The couple even hired a small team to handle day-to-day operations, freeing up their time to travel and spend quality time together.

On the topic of licensing, John's story stands out. A retired mechanical engineer, John invented a unique tool for gardening, securing a patent for it. Instead of manufacturing and selling it himself, he licensed it to a well-known gardening tools company. The agreement allowed John to receive royalties for every unit sold. This arrangement has made his retirement years not only comfortable but also quite luxurious. He now enjoys a steady income without lifting a finger to produce or market the tool himself.

Even more technologically aligned, there's Lisa, who invested in vending machines. Initially skeptical, she bought her first machine to see how it would go. Placing it strategically in a busy office building, she soon noticed a consistent income stream. Encouraged by her success, Lisa expanded to 50 machines across different locations in her city. The entire business is automated, with a service provider restocking the machines and handling maintenance. Each month, Lisa enjoys a significant passive income while dedicating her time to other interests.

Eric from California found success by investing in Real Estate Investment Trusts (REITs). These investments allowed him to earn without the hassles of direct property ownership. By carefully selecting REITs focusing on commercial real estate, Eric started receiving quarterly dividends. Over time, he diversified his REIT portfolio, making his passive income streams more stable and lucrative. Now, he spends his days mentoring young investors while his REIT investments continue to provide a substantial income.

Finally, let's talk about Dan, who capitalized on the growing trend of online courses. A former high school teacher, Dan designed an online curriculum for homeschooling parents. Partnering with a popular e-learning platform, he launched his first course. The reception was phenomenal, prompting him to create multiple courses covering different subjects. The passive income from course enrollments now surpasses his teaching salary, allowing Dan to focus on creating even more educational content.

Each of these stories is a testament to the power of passive income. They show that regardless of your background, education, or initial capital, there's potential to build a stream of revenue that requires minimal ongoing effort. Whether you're interested in real estate, stocks, digital products, or unique business ideas, there's a pathway to success.

Chapter 13:
The Future of Passive Income

Looking ahead, the landscape of passive income is poised for tremendous evolution, driven by rapid technological advancements and shifting economic paradigms. Blockchain technology, for instance, promises to revolutionize transparency and streamline passive income streams via decentralized finance (DeFi) and smart contracts. Similarly, the growth of e-commerce and digital products continues to create boundless opportunities for automated income. Don't overlook the potential in emerging fields like renewable energy credits, where savvy investments could yield impressive returns while contributing to a sustainable future. Keeping an eye on these trends isn't just wise; it's essential for staying ahead and ensuring your passive income strategies remain resilient in an ever-changing world.

Emerging Trends

The world of passive income is not static; it's continually evolving. With advancements in technology, shifts in the global economy, and changing consumer behaviors, new trends are emerging that can reshape how we think about and pursue passive income streams. These trends present enormous opportunities for those willing to adapt and capitalize on them.

Cryptocurrencies and Blockchain: Cryptocurrencies like Bitcoin and Ethereum are not just buzzwords anymore; they're becoming legitimate ways to generate passive income. With mechanisms like staking and yield farming, investors can earn returns simply by holding or utilizing their digital assets. Staking, in particular, involves locking up crypto to support blockchain operations and earning rewards in return. Yield farming takes this a step further by allowing users to lend their crypto assets through decentralized platforms and earn interest.

Then there's the concept of decentralized finance (DeFi), which removes the middleman from traditional financial systems, enabling peer-to-peer transactions. DeFi platforms offer various opportunities, including earning interest on crypto holdings, participating in liquidity pools, and even engaging in decentralized autonomous organizations (DAOs) to earn tokens. What may have seemed esoteric a few years ago is now a frontier with promising prospects.

Fractional Real Estate Investing: Real estate has long been a favored route for generating passive income, but the barriers to entry can be high. Fractional real estate platforms break down these barriers by allowing investors to buy shares of real estate properties. This means you can invest in a portion of a high-value property without needing the capital to buy it outright. Such platforms offer the potential for rental income and property appreciation while diversifying risk since you're not tied to a single property.

Royalties from Digital Content: Among the more exciting emerging trends in passive income is earning royalties from digital content. Platforms like YouTube, Spotify, and even niche subscription services allow content creators to monetize their work. Royalties aren't limited to music and videos; eBooks, online courses, and stock photography also offer avenues for passive earnings. The creation may require initial effort, but the income streams can be long-lasting.

Automated Online Businesses: The rise of AI and automation tools has revolutionized online businesses. From automated e-commerce stores to AI-driven customer service, technology can handle various business operations, freeing up your time and generating income with minimal manual intervention. Think chatbots that can manage customer inquiries 24/7, inventory management software that automatically restocks popular items, and even AI marketing tools that fine-tune ad campaigns for maximum ROI. This automation doesn't just reduce the workload; it can also make the business more efficient and scalable.

Sustainable and Ethical Investments: Another trend gaining traction is investing in sustainable and ethical businesses. Many investors now seek options that align with their values, focusing on renewable energy, ethical supply chains, and sustainable agriculture. These investments aren't just good for the planet; they often come with favorable returns as consumer demand for ethical products grows. Think solar energy companies, green tech startups, and even agriculture firms using sustainable practices.

Subscription-Based Models: The subscription economy is booming. From streaming services like Netflix and Spotify to monthly product boxes and software as a service (SaaS), businesses are increasingly adopting subscription models to generate steady income. As an investor, identifying and supporting companies with strong subscription bases can be lucrative. Better yet, creating a subscription service yourself—whether it's a newsletter, a membership club, or access to exclusive digital content—can be a consistent revenue generator.

AI-Created Content: Artificial Intelligence is not just managing businesses; it's generating content. AI tools can now write articles, create digital artwork, and even compose music. If leveraged properly, these tools can be used to generate passive income. For instance, AI could maintain a blog or social media page, creating content that draws in advertising revenue. While the concept might sound futuristic, several platforms already offer these services, making them more accessible than ever.

Peer-to-Peer Lending: Traditional loans are becoming less dominant as peer-to-peer (P2P) lending platforms rise in popularity. These platforms connect borrowers with individual lenders, often offering better rates for both parties. As an investor, you can lend money to individuals or small businesses and earn interest. The risk can be higher than traditional savings accounts, but the returns often are too, making it worth considering as part of a diversified portfolio.

Live-Streaming and Virtual Events: With the explosion of remote work and virtual interactions, live-streaming and virtual events have seen unprecedented growth. Content creators and professionals can monetize live streams through platforms like Twitch, YouTube Live, and even Facebook. Virtual events, from webinars to online conventions, also offer monetization opportunities through ticket sales and sponsorships. This new form of passive income allows individuals to leverage their expertise and passions in ways that were not possible before.

Metaverse Real Estate: The concept of virtual worlds—collectively known as the Metaverse—is becoming increasingly mainstream. Within these digital realms, virtual real estate is being bought, sold, and rented out. Platforms like Decentraland and The Sandbox offer users the chance to own a piece of the virtual world and monetize it through leasing, advertising, or creating virtual experiences. It's a speculative market but one with significant growth potential as our online and offline lives continue to merge.

We've seen how digital and decentralized finance is transforming passive income opportunities. However, staying ahead of these trends requires continuous learning and adaptability. Keeping an eye on developments like regulatory changes in cryptocurrency or advancements in AI tools can help you spot opportunities before they become mainstream.

So, what's next? While nobody can predict the future with certainty, understanding these emerging trends will undoubtedly provide a competitive edge. Whether it's diving into cryptocurrencies, exploring fractional ownership models, or investing in sustainable ventures, the future of passive income is bright and full of possibilities. With the right approach, you can turn these emerging trends into lasting income streams, giving you more freedom and financial security.

How to Stay Ahead of the Curve

As we find ourselves at the intersection of technological advancement and evolving market dynamics, it's crucial to continually adapt and innovate to maintain a competitive edge in the realm of passive income. Passive income isn't static; what works today might become irrelevant tomorrow. To stay ahead of the curve, one must be both vigilant and proactive in exploring and implementing new strategies and technologies.

First and foremost, never underestimate the power of ongoing education. Keeping yourself updated with the latest trends, laws, and investment opportunities is essential. Whether through online courses, podcasts, or industry conferences, make it a point to continually educate yourself. The financial sector is rife with innovation, from blockchain technology to artificial intelligence; knowing how these developments could impact passive income streams keeps you one step ahead.

Networking is another vital component. Surround yourself with like-minded individuals who are also focused on developing passive income streams. Join online communities, attend meetups, and engage in discussions on platforms like LinkedIn or specialized forums.

Through these connections, you'll gain insights and tips that might not be readily available elsewhere. Networking isn't just about what you know; it's also about who you know.

Diversification remains a key principle. Don't place all your eggs in one basket. Spread your investments across different passive income opportunities such as real estate, dividend stocks, online businesses, and more. This diversity can safeguard you against market volatility and ensure a more stable income flow. Additionally, each income stream may have its own cycle of profitability; balancing them can lead to long-term success.

Another step is leveraging technological advancements. Automation tools and software can greatly enhance your ability to manage multiple streams of income efficiently. From automated trading platforms for stocks to property management software for real estate, technology can save you time and reduce the risk of human error. Beyond automation, consider emerging technologies like blockchain for secure and transparent transactions or the Internet of Things (IoT) for smarter property management.

Flexibility and adaptability should be your mantras. The ability to pivot when something isn't working, or when a new opportunity arises, can make a world of difference. Be open to experimenting with new types of passive income that you might not have considered before. For instance, peer-to-peer lending and crowdfunding platforms have gained popularity and can be lucrative if approached correctly.

In the digital age, data is gold. Utilise analytics to monitor and optimise your passive income streams. Whether it's tracking website traffic for an e-commerce business, analyzing dividend yields, or assessing property valuations, data-driven decisions are often more effective. Familiarize yourself with basic data analysis tools or consider hiring experts who can provide deeper insights.

Risk management is another critical aspect. Diversification helps, but it's also essential to have a solid risk management plan. This includes regular reviews of your investment portfolio, being mindful of economic indicators, and keeping an emergency fund. Additionally, insurance products tailored to your investments, such as landlord insurance for rental properties, can offer an added layer of security.

Keeping an eye on emerging markets can also be a game-changer. While traditional markets in the U.S., Europe, or Japan often offer stability, emerging markets can offer higher returns, albeit with higher risk. Countries in Southeast Asia, Africa, or Latin America are developing rapidly and can present unique opportunities for passive income. Make sure to conduct thorough research and perhaps start with smaller investments to understand the nuances of these markets.

Social media presence isn't just for influencers; it's becoming increasingly important for all types of businesses. A strong online presence can drive traffic to your blog, e-commerce store, or any digital product you create. Invest time in understanding SEO (Search Engine Optimization) and social media marketing. The digital landscape is crowded, but with the right strategies, you can carve out a niche for yourself.

In addition to all the technical strategies, developing a resilient mindset is equally important. Success in passive income requires long-term thinking and perseverance. You'll face setbacks, and not every venture will be successful. The ability to learn from failures and continue pushing forward is often what separates successful passive income earners from the rest.

Ethical considerations should not be overlooked. Engaging in passive income streams that are sustainable and ethical can not only bring in profits but also build a reputation that attracts better opportunities. Ethical investing, sustainable real estate, and responsible business practices can make a significant impact not just on your wallet, but also on your conscience and the broader community.

Mentorship can be invaluable. Learning from those who have already succeeded in establishing solid passive income streams can provide you with unique perspectives and shortcuts to success. Seek out mentors who are willing to share their experiences and advice. Often, the real-world wisdom they impart can be more beneficial than theoretical knowledge.

Lastly, never lose sight of the bigger picture. Yes, passive income is about financial freedom, but it should also align with your broader life goals and values. Regularly reassess your objectives and ensure that your passive income strategies are propelling you towards your ideal life. Financial gains mean little if they don't contribute to your overall happiness and well-being.

By focusing on education, diversification, technology, flexibility, data analytics, risk management, emerging markets, a strong online presence, resilience, ethical considerations, mentorship, and your broader life goals, you can stay ahead of the curve in the ever-evolving landscape of passive income. The journey is dynamic and requires constant vigilance, but the rewards of staying ahead are well worth the effort.

Chapter 14:
Building Your Community

Your network is more than just a safety net; it's the fabric that can hold together your dreams of passive income. By connecting with like-minded individuals, you're not just filling up a rolodex, you're curating a community of potential collaborators, mentors, and even customers or clients. Sharing knowledge, resources, and encouragement accelerates everyone's journey. Think of it as a two-way street where generosity and curiosity pay off in spades. Attend local meetups, engage in online forums, and don't shy away from offering your expertise freely. The stronger your community, the more robust your passive income streams will become, weaving a durable foundation for long-term financial freedom and perhaps even leaving a legacy of collective success.

Networking for Success

When it comes to creating reliable streams of passive income, your personal network can often be your most valuable asset. People, ideas, and opportunities flow through the connections you nurture, turning an isolated attempt into a communal effort. Networking doesn't just open doors; it builds bridges to new ventures, partnerships, and insights that you might not access otherwise.

First, you've got to recognize that genuine networking is more than just collecting business cards. It's about building meaningful relationships founded on mutual benefit. These relationships are not limited to professional settings. Friends, family, and acquaintances can all be part of your network if you cultivate the connections with care. Every interaction you have is an opportunity to network, even if it doesn't appear to be one at first glance.

So, where do you start? The key lies in attending events that attract like-minded individuals. These could range from industry conferences to online forums to casual meet-ups and social gatherings. At these events, don't be shy; introduce yourself, show interest in others' experiences, and share your aspirations honestly. Don't forget to exchange contact information and follow up shortly after the meeting to keep the connection fresh. A simple message expressing your enthusiasm about the conversation can go a long way.

However, your online presence is just as critical. Platforms like LinkedIn, Facebook Groups dedicated to your niche, or even blogging communities can serve as fertile ground for networking. When you engage online, ensure your profile is not just complete but also engaging and reflective of your personality and professional ethos. Participate actively in discussions, contribute valuable content, and don't hesitate to send personalized connection requests to people who intrigue you. The goal here is to be visible and valuable without seeming like you're merely out to collect contacts.

One tactic to consider is hosting your own events. This could be something as grand as a seminar or as simple as a themed dinner party at your home. By creating spaces where meaningful interactions can happen, you naturally position yourself as a connector and a person of interest within the community. You'll not only expand your network but also deepen the relationships within it.

There's also something inherently valuable about helping others achieve their goals. You'd be surprised at how often assisting someone with advice, a contact, or even just a listening ear can circle back to benefit you. Networking is reciprocal by nature, and the more you give, the more you're likely to receive in terms of support, opportunities, and collaborations.

If you're looking to deepen relationships within your network, consider setting up regular meetings or check-ins. These don't have to be anything formal—a casual coffee chat or a quick video call can do wonders. Consistent interaction helps maintain a warm relationship and keeps you top-of-mind when new opportunities arise. Just as with personal relationships, professional connections require nurturing.

But let's not ignore the elephant in the room: not every networking attempt will be fruitful. Rejection and ghosting are part of the game, and it's crucial to not take these personally. Learn from each experience and refine your approach accordingly.

For those specializing in specific passive income streams, joining niche-specific groups can focus your networking efforts. If you're into real estate, real estate investment clubs and forums can be incredibly resourceful. For stock market enthusiasts, webinars and financial educational seminars can link you with professionals who have decades of experience. Bloggers and online entrepreneurs can benefit from masterminds and content creator conferences.

Networking for success is about creating a support system that empowers you to achieve your financial goals. The people you surround yourself with can inspire, mentor, and even partner with you on your passive income journey. And remember, while face-to-face interactions hold their weight, don't underestimate the potential of digital networking, especially in today's increasingly connected world.

In conclusion, the power of networking in building your community around passive income streams cannot be overstated. Whether you're shaking hands at a local networking event or sharing insights in an online group, the relationships you build are invaluable. They provide not just opportunities but also the support and motivation you need to stay the course. After all, financial freedom is not just about the money you make but also the people who help you get there.

Creating Impact with Your Wealth

When we talk about "Creating Impact with Your Wealth," it's not just about throwing money around. It's about using your resources thoughtfully to make a real difference. Imagine turning your accumulation of wealth into opportunities for those around you. How you can enrich your community, contribute to its growth, and leave a lasting footprint.

Let's break it down. Creating impact doesn't have to mean grand gestures. Sometimes, it's the small, consistent efforts that lead to significant change. First, consider what your community needs. Is it a better education system? More recreational facilities? Health services? Identifying these gaps is the initial step toward impactful giving.

Wealth in a community can have a snowball effect. By investing in local businesses, you're not only helping entrepreneurs but also creating jobs and fostering a thriving local economy. Think about the little coffee shop down the street that could really use a break or the burgeoning tech startup that just needs a bit of capital to go to the next level. Your investments can mean the difference between their success and struggle.

Now, let's talk about education. Funding scholarships and educational programs can have a generational impact. It's like planting a seed today that will grow into a forest tomorrow. When you give someone the chance to learn and improve their skills, you're investing in the future workforce and leaders of your community. Maybe it's as simple as donating to local schools or as complex as starting your own educational foundation.

Don't underestimate the power of healthcare. Good health is the bedrock of a productive community. Supporting local clinics, mental health services, or even organizing health camps can yield enormous benefits. Your contribution can lead to healthier lives, which in turn means a more productive and vibrant community. It's like hitting an invisible 'refresh' button on the community's well-being.

The arts often get overlooked, but they are crucial for a community's soul. Theater, music, and visual arts can transform and uplift. Fund local artists, sponsor community theaters, support public art installations. When people engage with art, it fosters creativity and unity. It's the emotional glue that binds people together.

Let's not forget about assisting the underprivileged. Sometimes the most immediate need is relief for those struggling the most. Offering financial support to shelters, food banks, and counseling services can help people get back on their feet. It's about creating an inclusive community where everyone feels they have a stake.

You might be wondering how to get started. It's simpler than it seems. Start small, with something manageable. Perhaps you're good at organizing—so organize a community event. Maybe your strength is networking—use it to connect people who can benefit each other. If you've got financial resources, leverage them strategically by partnering with local nonprofits who share your vision.

Remember, impact also comes from collaboration. Work with other like-minded individuals and organizations. Join clubs, become a member of charitable boards, or just attend local government meetings. Engage in conversations that matter. When powerful minds and resources come together, the effects are compounded.

Digital platforms also offer unique opportunities. Crowdfunding platforms, social media outreach, and online community groups can spread the word and gather support for your initiatives. It's an effective way to reach a broader audience quickly, and it's less resource-intensive than traditional methods.

It's also important to measure the impact of your efforts. Are educational outcomes improving? Is the local economy more robust? Are healthcare services now more accessible? Keeping track of these indicators helps you understand what's working and where you might need to pivot.

Moreover, creating impact isn't a one-time thing. It's an ongoing commitment. The needs of a community can change, and so should your strategy. Make it a habit to assess and reassess periodically. Regularly check in with the community to understand their evolving needs.

Don't shy away from sharing your story and successes. People are often inspired to contribute themselves when they see the change you've been able to make. Transparency can breed more involvement, more ideas, and more resources flowing into the areas that need them the most.

Finally, personal satisfaction and fulfillment are tremendous by-products of creating impact with your wealth. Knowing that you're playing a role in bettering your community brings a sense of purpose and joy that's hard to find elsewhere. It's a win-win—you're not just nurturing the community, but also experiencing growth and enrichment in your own life.

Creating impact with your wealth is more than just an expectation or responsibility; it's an opportunity to shape the kind of world you want to live in. It's about weaving the fabric of a community that's not just richer in terms of money, but in terms of culture, health, and happiness. So, start today and watch your efforts ripple outward, touching lives and making a real, lasting difference.

Chapter 15:
Maintaining Balance

In the whirlwind of building multiple streams of passive income, it's easy to get caught up in the hustle and lose sight of what truly matters: maintaining balance. Yes, you want financial freedom, but it's just as crucial to savor the journey. Trust me, juggling real estate deals, stock market investments, and online ventures can feel overwhelming if you're not tending to your well-being. Remember, staying motivated isn't just about the dollars and cents; it's about ensuring you have the mental bandwidth to enjoy your hard-earned success. Whether it's setting aside time for leisurely walks, indulging in hobbies, or just unplugging for a while, finding that sweet spot between work and relaxation will keep you vibrant and stress-free. It's not only essential for your mental health but will also give you the clarity to make smarter, more deliberate decisions. In this chapter, we'll dig deep into effective strategies for maintaining that crucial balance, so you never feel burned out or detached from the thrill of life.

The Importance of Work-Life Balance

Work-life balance is more than just a trendy buzzword; it's a cornerstone for sustainable success, especially when you're building passive income streams. Balancing work with personal life isn't just about having more free time; it's about ensuring that your work doesn't consume you, leaving room for other essential aspects of your life. As you embark on the journey of creating passive income, maintaining this equilibrium becomes even more critical.

Imagine this: you've succeeded in establishing multiple passive income streams. Perhaps you have rental properties bringing in monthly income, dividend stocks paying out quarterly, and an online business that sells digital products while you sleep. At first glance, it may seem like you've achieved the ultimate dream. However, without proper balance, even passive income can turn into a source of stress. Suddenly, you find yourself managing tenants' needs, keeping up with market trends, and updating your online business, all while your personal life takes a back seat.

The risk of burnout is real, even for activities labeled as 'passive'. The element of balance is crucial not only for your mental health but also for sustaining these income streams in the long run. If you're constantly working, you could lose sight of why you started this journey in the first place: to achieve financial freedom and enjoy life. Remember, the goal isn't just to make money but to make money work for you, providing you the time to pursue hobbies, spend time with family, and engage in self-care.

Creating a schedule can be a game-changer when it comes to work-life balance. Allocate specific hours for work tasks and personal activities. Make sure to stick to it. Sometimes, it's tempting to answer work emails late at night, but setting boundaries is essential. This habit helps in clearly delineating where work ends, and personal space begins. Try to designate a workspace at home to maintain a physical boundary. When you're not in this space, you're mentally off-duty.

Automation plays a significant role in maintaining balance. The tools and technologies available today make it easier to handle mundane tasks with minimal human intervention. Automation software can manage your emails, social media posts, and even financial transactions. By leveraging these tools, you free up time and mental bandwidth, reducing the day-to-day stress of managing your passive income sources. Think of tools like scheduling apps, automated marketing systems, and even property management software that alerts you to essential tasks. These tools are like having an invisible assistant that works round the clock, allowing you more downtime.

One often overlooked aspect of work-life balance is emotional well-being. Investing mentally and emotionally in work can take a toll over time. Mindfulness practices, such as meditation and yoga, can help you stay grounded and focused. These practices enhance your ability to handle stress and improve your concentration when you are working. Adding short breaks throughout your workday to practice mindfulness can yield significant benefits. Sometimes, stepping away from your tasks and taking deep breaths can offer a fresh perspective and renewed energy.

Social connections also play an invaluable part in maintaining balance. Reconnecting with family and friends helps to recharge your emotional batteries. Regular social interactions allow you to take a mental break from work-related activities and engage in meaningful conversations and experiences. These social bonds act as a safety net that helps cushion the emotional ups and downs associated with managing multiple income streams.

Furthermore, don't underestimate the power of hobbies and leisure activities. Whether it's painting, hiking, or playing a musical instrument, engaging in activities that you love can be incredibly rejuvenating. These activities serve as a creative outlet, relieving stress and providing a sense of fulfillment that work alone can't offer. It's essential to remember that happiness derived from hobbies carries over into your work life, making you more productive and motivated.

Physical health should also be a priority. Regular exercise, nutritious meals, and adequate rest are non-negotiable elements of a balanced life. Physical activity releases endorphins, which act as natural stress relievers. Exercise routines can be as simple as a morning jog, a gym session, or even a dance class. Balanced nutrition supports mental clarity and efficiency. Lastly, adequate sleep ensures that you're at your best both mentally and physically. These aspects are fundamental yet often overlooked in the hustle of maintaining passive income streams.

Another critical element of maintaining work-life balance is knowing when to delegate. You can't do everything yourself, no matter how efficient you might be. Hiring professionals or outsourcing tasks can significantly reduce your workload. For instance, hiring a property manager for your real estate investments can save considerable time and stress. Similarly, hiring a financial advisor or automation specialist can help you manage your investments more efficiently. Delegation allows you to focus on what you do best while leaving other tasks to experts.

Reflection and assessment are essential practices for maintaining balance. Regularly take a step back and evaluate your life. Are your work tasks intruding on your personal time? Is your stress level affecting your relationships or health? Asking these questions can help you identify imbalances early and take corrective action. Regular assessments help ensure that you're not just creating income but also living a fulfilling life.

Flexibility in your work schedule can go a long way in achieving balance. Unlike a 9 to 5 job, managing passive income streams allows for some degree of flexibility. You can tailor your work hours around your personal life rather than the other way around. If you have young children, consider working during their school hours. If you're an early bird, get your work done in the mornings to have the afternoons free for leisure or family activities. Taking advantage of this flexibility can make a significant difference in your overall well-being.

Finally, it's crucial to celebrate your achievements, no matter how small they may seem. Taking the time to acknowledge your successes provides a sense of accomplishment and motivation to keep going. Celebrations don't have to be grand; it could be as simple as taking a day off to enjoy a favorite activity or a family outing. These moments of joy and recognition make the hard work worthwhile and keep you motivated for future endeavors.

In summary, the importance of work-life balance cannot be overstated, especially when managing passive income streams. A balanced life contributes to sustained success, better mental and physical health, and ultimately, a more fulfilling and enjoyable life. By employing strategies like scheduling, automation, mindfulness, social connections, physical health, delegation, reflection, and celebrating achievements, you can create a harmonious balance between work and life. This balance will not only help you achieve financial freedom but also ensure that you genuinely enjoy the fruits of your labor.

Staying Motivated and Stress-Free

Finding ways to develop passive income streams demands not just intellectual and financial investment but also emotional endurance and mental clarity. It's essential to remember that while the nature of passive income is designed to be less hands-on once established, the journey to that point can be labor-intensive and emotionally taxing. Knowing how to stay motivated and manage stress effectively is critical to maintaining balance and ultimately achieving your financial goals.

One key aspect of staying motivated is keeping your "why" at the forefront of every decision and action. Ask yourself why you embarked on this journey in the first place. Was it for financial independence, more free time, or the ability to support your family? Having this clear vision in mind can reignite your passion and keep you pushing through tough times. Write down your "why" and place it somewhere visible, like on your fridge or desk, to serve as a constant reminder.

Managing stress starts with self-awareness. Being mindful of your stress levels and recognizing the symptoms early can help you take action before it becomes overwhelming. Take regular breaks during your workday to stretch, breathe, and reset. Don't underestimate the power of a five-minute pause to recharge your batteries. This can be as simple as stepping outside for some fresh air, doing a quick meditation, or enjoying a cup of coffee without any electronic distractions.

Another powerful tool for maintaining motivation is setting small, attainable goals. Break down your larger objectives into smaller, manageable tasks. Celebrating these incremental victories can provide a sense of progress and accomplishment. It's much like climbing a mountain; focusing on each small step rather than the intimidating peak makes the journey seem more achievable.

Networking with like-minded individuals can also provide a significant boost to your motivation. Surround yourself with people who are on similar journeys or have already achieved what you're striving for. Sharing experiences, challenges, and successes can provide not only practical advice but also emotional support. Consider joining online forums, attending webinars, or participating in local meet-ups.

Physical health plays a substantial role in managing stress and maintaining motivation. Regular exercise, a balanced diet, and sufficient sleep are foundational. Physical activity releases endorphins, which are natural stress relievers. Whether it's a morning jog, a yoga session, or even a dance class, find something that keeps you moving and stick to it. Remember, a healthy body supports a healthy mind.

The importance of hobbies and leisure activities can't be overstated. These activities can provide a much-needed escape from the grind and refresh your mind. Whether it's painting, gardening, cooking, or reading, make sure to carve out time for things you love. Hobbies can reignite your creativity, a vital component in finding innovative solutions to challenges you may face on your journey.

Mindfulness practices such as meditation and journaling can drastically reduce stress and enhance concentration. Meditation helps to center your thoughts and bring you back to the present moment, away from worries and anxieties about the future. Journaling, on the other hand, allows for the release of pent-up emotions and the organization of thoughts. It's a therapeutic way to clear mental clutter, leaving you more focused and energized for your work.

Regularly reviewing your progress is crucial for staying motivated. Take time to reflect on how far you've come and what you've achieved. Sometimes, in the rush to achieve more, we forget to acknowledge our growth. Keeping a journal or a progress tracker can be incredibly helpful. These reflections can provide a much-needed boost when you're feeling stuck or demotivated.

It's also essential to be flexible and adaptable. The path to passive income is rarely linear. There will be twists and turns, and you need to be prepared for them. Being rigid in your approach can lead to unnecessary stress. Instead, view challenges as opportunities for growth. Adapting and evolving based on what you learn along the way will keep you resilient and motivated.

Often, the stress we experience comes from self-imposed pressures and unrealistic expectations. It's crucial to manage these by setting realistic timelines and being kind to yourself. Acknowledge that it's okay to take longer than expected and that setbacks are a natural part of the journey. Being compassionate towards yourself can reduce stress and keep you motivated.

Experimenting with different productivity techniques can keep your work both efficient and enjoyable. The Pomodoro Technique, for example, involves working in focused bursts with short breaks in between. This method can improve concentration and provide regular intervals for relaxation, helping to manage stress. Another strategy is the two-minute rule: if a task takes two minutes or less, do it immediately. This can prevent minor tasks from piling up and becoming overwhelming.

Delegate whenever possible. You don't have to do everything on your own. If hiring someone to handle repetitive or time-consuming tasks is within your budget, it can be a worthwhile investment. Delegating not only reduces your workload but also allows you to focus on higher-level tasks that require your unique skills and creativity. This can significantly reduce stress and maintain your motivation.

Learning and personal development should always be part of your routine. The more you know, the easier it is to navigate challenges and leverage opportunities. Make it a habit to read books, take online courses, or listen to podcasts related to passive income and personal growth. Staying curious and continually expanding your knowledge will keep you engaged and motivated.

Lastly, never underestimate the power of positivity and gratitude. Keeping a gratitude journal where you jot down things you're thankful for each day can shift your mindset from stress and scarcity to abundance and positivity. A positive outlook fosters creativity and problem-solving, essential traits for anyone on the path to building passive income.

Developing passive income streams is a transformative journey, one fraught with ups and downs. Staying motivated and stress-free isn't just about working diligently towards your goals, but also about nurturing your well-being along the way. By incorporating these practices into your routine, you'll not only achieve financial success but also enjoy a balanced and fulfilling life.

The Journey to Financial Freedom

The path to financial independence isn't a straight line. It's more like a winding road, full of unexpected curves and detours. Yet, each twist and turn carries its own lessons, enriching the journey. As we've explored throughout this book, building passive income streams is one of the keys to attaining true financial freedom. Whether it's investing in real estate, diving into dividend stocks, or venturing into online businesses, the avenues are varied and plentiful.

One of the first steps in this journey is rethinking what it means to work. Traditional wisdom often equates hard work with long hours, but passive income challenges that notion. It's about smart work, strategic investments, and consistent, calculated efforts. When we cultivate passive income sources, we're not just looking for escape routes from the nine-to-five grind; we're creating systems that generate revenue without constant oversight.

The transformation begins at a psychological level. Realizing the potential of passive income brings an ideological shift. No longer do we see income purely as a product of labor; instead, we start to view it as a flow stemming from wise choices and sound investments. This new perspective empowers us to take calculated risks, innovate, and expand our horizons. The end result is a diversified portfolio that provides financial stability and a sense of accomplishment.

This book has covered an array of passive income streams, each with its pros and cons. From the solidity of real estate investments to the dynamism of online businesses, the choices are numerous. But what

Josephine Goody

truly matters is picking what aligns with your unique skills and goals. No one-size-fits-all formula exists. Therefore, your journey will be uniquely yours, tailored to your preferences, competencies, and ambitions.

An important aspect of achieving financial freedom is setting realistic and actionable goals. This is something we discussed at length in the chapter on setting financial goals. Remember: it's crucial to balance short-term wins with long-term visions. Meaningful progress often comes from a series of small, consistent actions. Breaking down your grand vision into manageable tasks makes the entire process less daunting and more attainable.

Real estate investment is frequently touted as the linchpin of passive income. For good reason, too. When done prudently, it offers tangible and substantial returns. But it's not without its challenges—market fluctuations, property management, and regulatory hurdles can pose difficulties. However, these hurdles are surmountable with the right knowledge and resources, transforming real estate into a reliable source of passive income.

The stock market, particularly through dividend stocks, provides another robust avenue for passive income. Building a dividend stock portfolio requires an understanding of market dynamics and a knack for selecting dividend-paying companies with consistent performance. With careful planning, it's possible to create a portfolio that offers a steady stream of income, adding a valuable layer of financial security.

In the digital age, becoming an online entrepreneur offers unparalleled opportunities. From e-commerce ventures to affiliate marketing, the potential is massive. Creating digital products such as eBooks, courses, or software can cater to niche markets while generating recurring revenue. The initial effort required to set up these ventures might be substantial, but the ongoing maintenance can be minimal, leading to significant passive income over time.

134

When setting out on this journey, automation should be at the forefront of your strategy. Automating tasks—be it through software tools or outsourcing—frees up time for more strategic decision-making. Automation doesn't just streamline operations; it also bolsters productivity, laying the foundation for scalable passive income streams.

Managing these sources of passive income is another critical aspect that can't be overlooked. Keeping track of investments, calculating returns, and staying on top of taxes are ongoing responsibilities that ensure your financial ecosystem remains healthy. Neglecting these tasks can quickly turn potential gains into losses, underscoring the need for diligent management.

As you amass experience and success, scaling up your passive income streams becomes the next logical step. Whether by diversifying your investments or increasing stakes in high-yield ventures, scaling ensures that your income grows along with your ambitions. However, it's essential to exercise caution and avoid overextending yourself. Each growth phase should be backed by solid research and sound financial strategies.

Every journey encounters pitfalls, and the quest for financial freedom is no different. From market volatility to unforeseen expenses, setbacks will arise. The chapter on common mistakes and overcoming setbacks provides valuable insights on how to navigate these challenges. Resilience and adaptability are key traits that will see you through difficult times, turning obstacles into stepping stones.

Hearing success stories can be incredibly motivating. They show that the journey to financial freedom is not merely theoretical but attainable. The stories we've shared range from humble beginnings to significant financial triumphs, each underscoring the limitless possibilities that come with determination and strategic planning.

Looking ahead, the landscape of passive income is continually evolving. Emerging trends in technology and market behavior offer fresh opportunities. Staying ahead of the curve is crucial. Continuous learning and adaptation will keep you at the forefront, ensuring your passive income strategies remain viable in the face of change.

Building a community around your financial endeavors offers immense benefits. Networking introduces you to new opportunities, collaborations, and insights, all of which can enhance your financial journey. Moreover, financial freedom brings the ability to make a meaningful impact, be it through philanthropy, mentorship, or innovation. Your wealth becomes a tool for broader social benefits, creating a legacy beyond personal gain.

Remember, financial freedom isn't just about amassing wealth; it's about achieving balance. Work-life harmony, motivation, and stress management are crucial elements that sustain your journey. Achieving financial freedom without sacrificing quality of life is the ultimate goal. This balance is what truly transforms a financially free individual into a fulfilled one.

Your journey to financial freedom is unique, but it's grounded in universal principles of smart work, strategic planning, and continuous adaptation. As you embark on this path, remember that each step forward, no matter how small, brings you closer to a life of greater choice, security, and fulfillment. Embrace the challenges, celebrate the milestones, and keep your vision clear. Financial freedom is a journey worth taking, and it's one that will transform not just your finances, but your entire life.